Travel Back In Rhyme

The South East

Edited by Mark Richardson

First published in Great Britain in 2012 by:
YoungWriters
Remus House
Coltsfoot Drive
Peterborough
PE2 9BF
Telephone: 01733 890066
Website: www.youngwriters.co.uk

Book Design by Tim Christian

SB ISBN 978-0-85739-812-3

Foreword

Young Writers was established in 1991, dedicated to encouraging reading and creative writing by young people. Our nationwide writing initiatives are designed to inspire ideas and the incentive to write, and in turn develop literacy skills and confidence, whilst participating in a fun, imaginative activity. The final reward is the opportunity for thc budding young writer to see their work in print.

Our latest competition, Travel Back In Rhyme, focuses on using historical periods, events or people to inspire poetry. The resulting collection is an illuminating glimpse into the past through the eyes of our young generation. There is verse inspired by everything from dinosaurs and cavemen, to the ancient civilisations of Greece and Egypt, to the World Wars and even space travel. The talented young poets have created verse that is gory, funny, dramatic, tragic: a reflection of human history up to the present day.

Using a mix of imagination, expression and historical inspiration, this anthology is an impressive snapshot of the inventive, original and skilful writing of young people today. With the extra bonus of fun fact pages about some of history's best bits, this collection is a journey back in time that will delight readers for years to come.

Contents

The Poems

Caveman Hunt

In the morning bright and early
Papa caveman wakes us up.
The day has started fair and happy
The caveman's children jump and shout.

Fire crackles in the circle
Breakfast is upon the spit.
Let us sharpen all our weapons
Spears and arrows made of flint.

Mother waves the men farewell
'Courage, have no fear,' she cries.
Now the young ones can play
While they wait for supper to arrive.

There's the deer, the bow is drawn
Aim it well, you'll not be scorned.
Perfect shot, the deer falls dead
We drag it home, hold up our heads.

Mother shouts with jubilation
For at last food's on its way
Little ones cheer a loud hooray.

There they squat around the fire
Fingers eager for a taste.
Soon they've had all they desire
None at all will go to waste.

Mia Fischli (10)
Beech Grove School, Nonington

The Safety Of Fire

Spears ready for the kill
It's a mammoth near the hill
Drive it, stone it, poke it too
Victory, victory, victory

Come squat round the flames so bright
Come, oh come, to warmth and light
Come have meat, our supper's hot
Mammoth meat until you pop

Settle down around to sleep
Hoots and howls awake won't keep
Safe around the flames so bright
We will sleep all through the night.

Asha Hine (10)
Beech Grove School, Nonington

The Hunt

Men are creeping through the wood
Spears raised, ready to attack.
Where's the boar that they had seen?
'There he is!' the cry rings out.
Now the chase is on! Dash here
Sprint there, where's it gone?
He's here.
Come quick, kill him, get him now!
Now he is dead, haul him to camp,
Build up the fire, coals glow bright.
We have supper, pork tonight!
Yum . . yum . . . gurgle . . . gurgle . . . belch!

Jurisa Shirky (10)
Beech Grove School, Nonington

A Caveman's Life

When cavemen first discovered fire
They used it for both warmth and light.
The men made tools to hunt the game
The women scraped skins and cooked it right.
They mined the flint out of the ground
And chipped it sharp to make weapons sound.
The flint was chipped into arrowheads
And mounted on sticks to make spears of dread.
The cavemen painted on the walls
Scenes of hunting animals.

Erika Meier (10)
Beech Grove School, Nonington

The Fire Friend

Chipping flint makes sparks so bright
Fire gives food, warmth and light
When you draw close to flame
You will run right back again
Woolly mammoth roasting well
Hunks of meat that we impale
Moving onward through the Weald
We appoint a fire shield
Guard the fire and defend
Till we come to journey's end.

Agnes Comer (10)
Beech Grove School, Nonington

Fire Comes In Many Ways

Fire comes from erupting volcanoes,
Spilling crimson on the ground,
Fire comes from thunderstorms,
Lightning strikes a fire to found.
Fire comes from flint and steel.
Making sparks to leap alight.
Fire comes to warm and protect
Early man from cold and fright.

Brenda Kleinsasser
Beech Grove School, Nonington

A Caveman's Day

Cavemen hunting, gathering and fishing
Guarding camp, their fires watching
Roasting meat, their flint tools chipping
Bows and arrows and spears shaping
Pits for mammoths they are digging
With flint scrapers the hides they're skinning
Eating meat and drinking rain
A caveman's life is hard each day.

Zeke Maendel (10)
Beech Grove School, Nonington

The Peryton

The Peryton
Originally from Atlantis
Wicked, appalling, mystical
Like a golden eagle
Man-eating giant
Frightened the sailors hide
People so scared
They have no spirit within them
The Peryton
Slayer of sailors.

Maisie Cadd (10)
Bethersden Primary School, Bethersden

Champion Athletes

I can feel the wind in my face
Dust floating in my mouth
Crashing armour
Steel and leather
Crowds cheering
Finish line waiting
Hearts racing
Sweat dripping
Legs aching
Breathing deeply
Wanting to win
Dreams to clasp
Feet tiring
Athletes stumbling, falling
Dry mouth
Wanting water
Green eyes
Athletes pushing
Finish line braking.

Holly Spooner (9)
Bethersden Primary School, Bethersden

Horses Racing

Eager horses ready to win the race,
Athletes ready to win too
Athletes red and sweating
Horses galloping. Going fast
Horses' coats sweating
People shouting loudly
Hands bleeding and blistered
Horses nearly out of breath
They speed round the stadium like charging rhinos
Bullying their way to the finish line
Budging and pushing
Victory for the winner!

Joel Oliver (8)
Bethersden Primary School, Bethersden

Champion Of Champions

Armour clunking
Crowds cheering
Racers struggling
Finish line waiting, waiting
Heads sweating
Mouth bone dry
Hearts beating, beating
Legs tiring
Dreams ending
Athletes pushing
Feet aching, aching
Athletes tripping
Dust getting carried by the wind
Finish line nearing
Sprinting, sprinting
Want to win
Want a victory
Almost there!

Victoria Wratten Wood
Bethersden Primary School, Bethersden

Going For Gold

Athletes pacing together
Divers diving all over the place, like flying fish
The gun blasts, sprinters start
I'm going to win
Crowds shouting loudly
The crowd goes wild
The wind sweeps past me
Chariots hit one another
Sad people crying
The dreams broken
Going for gold
I'm legend
Finish line her I come
I won!

Daniel Rogers
Bethersden Primary School, Bethersden

Brown Racing Horses

The crowd went wild,
The horses groomed and ready
Steaming breath
Horse galloping fast
Trying to win.
Their hooves hitting the ground
Thumping sound,
Riders sweating.
I can smell horses' coats
The horses wanting for water
They're near the finishing line
Riders encouraging their horses to go faster
One horse, the fastest, was near the finish,
Then, he won!
The crowd cheered and shouted -
Gold for the victor!

Georgia Alard (8)
Bethersden Primary School, Bethersden

Chariot Racing

Hooves stamping
The flag is waving
Dust blowing in my face
Sweating faces racing past
The finishing line is waiting
Horses crashing into each other
Athletes wishing to win
Horses' hearts thumping wildly
The crowd is cheering
Chariots crash nearby
Wheels spinning
I'm scared, my victory disappearing
I am near the finish
Am I going to win?
Yes, I've won!
The prize is waiting.

Eleanor Fuller (8)
Bethersden Primary School, Bethersden

Horse Power

Horses' hooves
Heavy breath
Wheels spinning
Round and round
The track
I can hear
Them coming back

Crashing carts
Wheels flying
Round the track
I feel crash on my back

I had nearly reached the end of the track,
Until I crashed and hurt my back.

Finley Bryant
Bethersden Primary School, Bethersden

Race In Armour

Runners waiting
People cheering
Hearts thumping
The runners are off
Dust is everywhere
I can smell sweaty bodies
Runners running down the track
I can see people trying to win
Almost there
The crowd is screaming loudly
And the finish line is waiting.

Lauren Fletcher (9)
Bethersden Primary School, Bethersden

Harpies

Harpies -
Half woman, half bird,
Fearsome, cruel, terrifying,
Trapped serving the mighty gods,
Demons flying across the world,
Terrifying, swooping through the sky for their prey,
The people below are oblivious that they are there,
Harpies -
A mysterious threat from the sky.

Lauren Webber (9)
Bethersden Primary School, Bethersden

Cutting Water

On the diving board getting ready to jump
Heart pounding
Muscles quivering
Swimmers cutting through the water,
Sharp as a soldier's knife
Performance done
Cheering loudly
Scores to be given
Dreams won.

Riley Stolten (10)
Bethersden Primary School, Bethersden

The Kraken

The Kraken of legend, found at the end of the world
Dangerous, deadly, murderous
Big, dangerous squid in a colossal body,
As dangerous as rough seas,
A temper like an erupting volcano.
The Kraken has killed a thousand sailors,
I feel like running away and screaming -
The Kraken!

Adam Bray (10)
Bethersden Primary School, Bethersden

Runner's Hope

Runners at the ready
While the bullet shoots the sky
Tripping and tumbling
The sun covers the sky, burning its victims
Heels crashing to the ground
Finishing line waiting
For the runner who might claim the prize
People's dreams starting to crumble
Who will claim the victory?

Mia Padilla (9)
Bethersden Primary School, Bethersden

The Chimera

One half lion, the other half goat,
A terrifying creature, fierce,
Trapped in a dangerous place,
A fearsome mountain of rage,
Its strength terrifying,
It makes me feel like a tiny ant,
The Chimera,
Reminds us of how big life is.

Holly Bruty (10)
Bethersden Primary School, Bethersden

The Manticore

Deep within the Indian jungle
Vicious, poisonous, cruel
Trapped in a world of invasion
A fierce living rage
Terrified, the Greeks give way
It makes me feel like a minute bug
Deadly poisonous spines still trapped
In an invasive world.

Lucy Lerwill (10)
Bethersden Primary School, Bethersden

The Nereid

The Nereid, a sea nymph,
Beautiful and golden-haired,
Soft skin like a forest maiden,
Like an angel from Heaven.
It makes me lost in this big, big world,
Like an important person being ignored.
The Nereid.

Zoe Wilkinson (10)
Bethersden Primary School, Bethersden

Cerberus

Deep in the bowels of the Earth,
Shocking, fierce and dangerous;
Trapped by stolen souls,
Like a volcano erupting -
People who go near are petrified!
Cerberus,
Guardian of the underworld.

Caspar Aitken (10)
Bethersden Primary School, Bethersden

Battle Of Bosworth

Swords and shields slashing and bashing,
A passageway of dead bodies
Rotting more and more by the day.
Swords clashing and screaming for help,
Hooves thundering as they pass,
Frightening earthquake underneath,
Lumps on the ground where dead bodies have been kept.
The crashing of cannons, cannonballs on the ground,
Everyone is frightened of what's going to happen next
The dead corpses have been scented from all around,
The odour of smoke from cannonballs hitting the ground,
The stench of horses and fear floating through the air.

Evie Paine (10)
Brede Primary School, Rye

World War Two

Gunshots firing and injured soldiers shouting for help,
Medics rushing to heal the wounded.
Dead bodies scattered, a river of blood streaming through the field,
Tanks firing their shells and smashing the enemy.
Penetrating bullets putting holes through enemy helicopters.

Screaming voices echoing throughout the battlefield,
Thundering grenades hitting the ground
And blowing up so loud five soldiers went deaf.

The smoke from blown up enemy vehicles,
Poisonous gases fill the air.
The stench of rotting flesh and blood!

The ground rumbling as grenades explode,
Soldiers rushing and pushing past,
The cold, wet rain dripping on your face,
While the wet mud squishy and slippy.

The taste of mushy mud and smoke,
Warm water and cold, sloppy meals.
The soldiers lonely and depressed.
The soldiers scared but excited, all ready to fight.

Ben Reader (9)
Brede Primary School, Rye

World War Two

Gunshots deafening,
The floor trembling underfoot,
Planes crashing, tanks exploding,
Planes whizzing overhead,
People invading,
Protected by tanks from gunfire,
All you can see is horrifying planes and jeeps,
A massive mushroom cloud consuming the battlefield,
Gas bombs, people suffocating in trenches,
Guns spitting fire straight at you,
All you can do is fire back.

Hogarth Hannam (9)
Brede Primary School, Rye

The Battle

Thud! Thud!
Went the soldiers
Squelch! Squelch!
Went the mud
Shout! Shout!
Went the Romans
Clank! Clank!
Went the horse
Bang! Bang!
Went the swords
Pop! Pop!
Went the fire
Thump! Thud!
Went the soldiers marching
Clash! Clash!
Went the soldiers
Bump! Bump!
Went the soldiers
They all stopped everything forever.

Lucy Harvey (6)
Brede Primary School, Rye

Romans

Romans are fearless.
Romans are tough.
Romans never give up, their armour is shiny,
To them we look tiny, but we will stand mighty!

As their armour clashes and bashes,
As their sword clashes the sound of lashes in your ears,
Horses' hooves fall on you but the sound is thundering!

Our tiny army has walked so far,
Carrying out armour and shields,
Leaving our families to fight in this war.
Feeling like kings of the field,
But then again the feeling of triumph in our hearts!

Heather Smith (10)
Brede Primary School, Rye

The Battle

Stomp, stomp!
Went the soldiers' feet
Squidge, squidge!
Went the mud beneath their feet
Clang, clang!
Went the Roman swords
Thump, thump!
Went the soldiers of the Romans
Fling, fling!
Went the bows and arrows
Shuffle, shuffle!
Went the Roman soldiers shuffling into a line
Bark, bark!
Went the menacing dogs
Yeah, yeah!
Said the conquering Romans.

Ole Reader (8)
Brede Primary School, Rye

Woe For War

Alone and frightened children stand,
As their scruffy dog sits down in the sand,
Everyone looks at the destruction of the town,
Everyone's faces filled with frowns.

Personal things in houses, battered
And outside all the shops, bricks scattered,
Blocks of flats filled with fire,
All their hopes are not getting higher.

Air raid sirens sound like a little girl,
British planes come down with a curl.
Explosions and gunfire everywhere,
Every five minutes they see a crackling flare.

These scared little children are not going to play,
These scared little children are going to have a sorrow-filled day.

Nathan Acheson (10)
Brede Primary School, Rye

War

WW2 solider,
Gunshots firing, tanks rolling,
Thousands of men fighting for their lives.
Searching for enemy intel,
Men crossing enemy lines,
Jumping into action,
A front row seat to the goriest fight in history.

Gunpowder piercing ears,
C4 blowing jeeps into the air,
Banging bombs soaring,
42 caliber bullets.

Feeling scared and frightened,
Fear growing with a hint of excitement and joy
That your country is going to win.

Charlie Ithell (10)
Brede Primary School, Rye

The Fight

Clip, clop!
Went the horses' hooves
Thump, thump!
The soldiers marched
Clink, clink!
Went the soldiers' swords
Cry, cry!
From the Celtic warriors
Scratch, scratch!
As the shields rubbed together
Stomp, stomp!
Went the soldiers marching
Bang, bang!
The shields clashed

Oliver Leroy-Lewis (6)
Brede Primary School, Rye

Flaming Mayhem

Crack, crack!
Went the wood as it was set on fire
Fizz, fizz!
Went the flaming arrows
Bark, bark!
Went the dog
Sizzle, sizzle!
Went the fire
Huddle, huddle!
Went the Romans
Ouch, ouch!
Shouted the injured soldiers
Hooray, hooray!
Shouted the conquering Roman soldiers.

Tom Giles (9)
Brede Primary School, Rye

The Fighters

Ow, ow!
Went the man
Shuffle, shuffle!
As the man went along
Clip, clop!
As the horse went by
Clash, clash!
Went the heavy shields
Crunch, crunch!
As the men were marching
Clank, clank!
Went the swords,
Screech, screech!
Went the Celts.

James Wilson (7)
Brede Primary School, Rye

Romans Versus Celts

Ouch, ouch!
Went the stabbed soldiers
Clank, clank!
Went the swords
Bash, bash!
Went the shields
Crush, crush!
They fell on each other
Crunch, crunch!
Bones are broken
Clop, clop!
Went the horses' hooves
Bark, bark!
Went the nasty dogs

Honey Fox (7)
Brede Primary School, Rye

Romans Army Olympics

Clip, clop!
Went the horses' hooves
Clang, clang!
Goes the swords
Screech, screech!
Goes the leader
Stomp, stomp!
Went the Romans
Crunch, crunch!
Went the stones
Ouch, ouch!
Went the soldiers.

Alex Simmons (7)
Brede Primary School, Rye

The Sounds Of Battle

Clip, clop!
Went the horses' hooves
Clank, clank!
Went the swords
Thud, thud!
Went the sandals
Squelch, squelch!
Went the mud
Screech, screech!
Went the Celts
Yes! Yes!
Screamed the Romans.

Robbie Jones (7)
Brede Primary School, Rye

WW2

Gunshots firing at injured soldiers,
Tanks driving over downed soldiers,
Penetrating bullets punching holes in enemies tanks.

Booming cannons blowing up helicopters,
Hooves thundering on the muddy grass,
Exploding grenades getting thrown into bunkers.

Smoke from blown up bunkers,
Rotting flesh covered in flies and maggots,
Burning trees in the distance,
The ground trembling with bangs,
Helicopters crash landing on the ground.

Darrel Haire (9)
Brede Primary School, Rye

Roman Warriors

People slashing swords
While Romans protect their land.
Warriors come from corner to corner
Destroying everything in their paths.
Romans using horses to hunt down and slaughter.
Grass swaying while the warriors sit and wait for war to break loose.
When they win they sing a song of victory.

Joshua Carter (9)
Brede Primary School, Rye

Back To Tudor Times

I travelled back in time
I travelled to the Tudor time
I travelled to the Battle of Bosworth
I travelled to the sight of horrible death
I travelled to Tudor Times
I smelt a whiff of scared horses
I smelt what soldiers walk on
I smelt what you don't usually smell
I smelt Tudor times
I heard swords clashing
I heard high pitched screams
I heard what you don't usually hear
I heard Tudor times
I saw a sea of blood with dying fish, people
I saw an explosion of weapons
I saw Tudor times
I felt sad and crushed
I felt I should help, which side?
I felt what you don't usually feel
I felt Tudor times
Time to leave the dying people
Time to go back home
Time to leave the big adventure
Time to say goodbye to Tudor times.

Hendrikje Dorussen (9)
Broomgrove Junior School, Wivenhoe

Royal Tudors

Henry Tudor began the age
And the start of my new page
It's said that he beat Richard the Third
In a battle that was not absurd
He got the crown and the rose
Leaving Richard with the crows
Arthur Tudor was unwell
Good job he didn't go to Hell
Henry was the next that came
He said that Arthur was quite lame
He got himself a pretty wife
For twenty years of his life
But then one day he fell off his horse
That made him bad of course
He split up with Catherine, killed wife two
Married four more times, wouldn't you?
Edward Sixth was after him
His coronation was quite dim
He was unwell when he was crowned
He never lived long that's what we found
Lady Jane Grey was next to come
She came from nowhere says everyone
Mary I was second queen
And the scariest we have seen
The last Tudor was little Queen Liz
She really was quite the biz
She reigned the longest in Tudor days
For forty five years that's what she says
But unfortunately there was no heir
So the Tudor's reign had ended there.

Jim Gordon (9)
Broomgrove Junior School, Wivenhoe

Deafness Cure

I am ill and deaf
Yesterday I met
The gall from a hare
Then from a fair
I got grease from a fox
And kept them both in a box

Everyone saying put in your ear
No way, I say, I'll be deaf once more
Please, please is all I could hear
I have a lot of fear
I'd rather be deaf than have a death

It's terrible like this
At least it's better that being punched with a fist
I don't feel well
It's annoying having to ring my bell

Eventually I'm better
Now I'll write a letter
To my wonderful grandmother.

Megan Amy Ashley (10)
Broomgrove Junior School, Wivenhoe

Tudor Feasts

Tudor food, crunchy and soft,
Lifting you up aloft,
Tasty meals, such as
Beef, duck and fox.

Hungry people eating food
That smells sharp and smooth
Smelling like a sea breeze,
Acting refreshing and smooth.

Feeling like a palace rich
The food comes all on a dish
While everybody is enjoying their meal
With a large sense of appeal.

Milo Priest (10)
Broomgrove Junior School, Wivenhoe

Catherine Of Aragon's Divorce

C atherine of Aragon the doomed one
A t Richmond Castle
T he room fills with sadness
H ere there is nothing but misery
E ntirely sad, entirely bad
R oom filled with tears
I n the shadow of skulls -
N ow all I ask you is not to divorce me
E ntirely sorrowful is this day

O h Henry, your fake, loving heart
F or goodness sake, I didn't know I'd be cheated . . .

A morning of darkness
R aining down night
A t this doomed castle
G oing with a doomed mind
O n and on with misery forever -
N ow think about yourself Henry!

Lyra Klujber (9)
Broomgrove Junior School, Wivenhoe

Tudor Punishment

All I can see are people dying
What have they done wrong?
Killed in such a horrible way
Crime and punishment

All I can see are dead bodies
Cut off limbs
I can feel water splashed
From the ducking stool
Crime and punishment

All I can hear are screams
Shouts along with the sound
Of heads being chopped off
Crime and punishment.

Harry Hubert (10)
Broomgrove Junior School, Wivenhoe

Stepping Into A New World

Stepping into a new world
Seeing all scenery change,
The light turns from topaz to dust,
The furniture wooden range,
I see the world a different place,
Gloomy, lonely, musty.

Stepping into a new world,
See what I feel,
I feel the sorrow of a forlorn girl,
I feel how she longs for a meal,
I feel slow, but my mind a whirl.

Stepping into a new world,
Hearing the silence of the room,
Do I have to hear the surprised sound
Of the girl, wondering who
May be visiting her in her lonely world.

Iona Allen (9)
Broomgrove Junior School, Wivenhoe

Evacuation

I feel terrified
I feel scared
I feel shivery
I feel homesick
I feel hungry
I feel nervous

Waiting for the train
Brown leather bag
Big fat teddy

I feel lonely
I feel frightened

Where am I?
Where will I be?
Where will I sleep?

Jodi Waterman (7)
Broomgrove Junior School, Wivenhoe

Evacuation

Waiting for my name to be called out

Brown leather bag
Big, cuddly, warm coat
My favourite soft teddy
Woolly, cosy clothes
Four sandwiches
A wrecked old table.

How I feel -
Shivery,
Travel sick
Frightened.

Are you a criminal?
Are you a chimney sweeper?
What's your name,
Can my sister live with us?

Jasmine Whitting (7)
Broomgrove Junior School, Wivenhoe

On the Battlefield

Serious
Scared
Shocked
Suffocated
On the battlefield!
Revolting
Rowdy
Wrong
Ragged
On the battlefield!
Tremendous
Terrified
Terrible
Torture
On the battlefield!
And that is what you see on a battlefield.

Lucy Scott (9)
Broomgrove Junior School, Wivenhoe

Horrid Henry

Sport, sport, sport! says the king
He loves his dinner, ding, ding, ding
He has a lot of fans
With all his instruments he could make a band

After his injury to his leg, no more exercise
Just more pies
He needed a son
And a few more buns
For the lord's tum

King Henry, what a mean man
Not many were a fan
Even more now he's old
Everyone around felt icy cold.

Ben Creasey (9)
Broomgrove Junior School, Wivenhoe

The Awful Battle Of Bosworth

Screams and shouts filled the air
Blood and guts everywhere

Clanking armour on the knights
People falling off their horses
Hooves thundering whilst they gallop

Eyeballs on the floor
Brains on feet - stuck forever
I see lots of guts in front of me
Red hair from the blood

Screams and shouts filled the air
Blood and guts everywhere.

Rhianna Dickson (9)
Broomgrove Junior School, Wivenhoe

Crime And Punishment

All I can see are
Bright red tomatoes
Coming towards me

All I can hear are
People shouting horrible
Words at me

All I can feel
Is shame

A harsh, wooden
Punishment, the stocks.

Jessica Scott (9)
Broomgrove Junior School, Wivenhoe

Tudor Feast

I can see wine, meat vegetables, dancing
I can see King Henry with his wife, Anne Boleyn

I can feel the large tables
With wooden cutlery
With its pottery plates
With glass glasses, it's all lovely

I can hear music being played by a band so good
You can hear the band throughout the land
With shoes on the ground dancing through the night.

Oliver Barnard (9)
Broomgrove Junior School, Wivenhoe

The Death Of The Mary Rose

Bodies floating on the thick, crusty water
The Mary Rose upside down and sinking
The French laughing and proud of their work
The ship now dead and at the bottom of the greedy sea
The sea making the sound of a whirlpool.

Joshua Behn (10)
Broomgrove Junior School, Wivenhoe

Evacuation

Waiting for my mum and dad to say goodbye

Shivering from head to toe

I feel lonely

With my snugly hedgehog

Not happy

Homesick

Got my label stuck to my brown leather bag.

Megan Brown (7)
Broomgrove Junior School, Wivenhoe

Serving The Food

Rush, frantic, will it be right?
Rabbit, swan, pig's head.

Delicious, spectacular smells
Rabbit, swan, pig's head.

Dancers, happiness, food
Rabbit, swan, pig's head.

Rowdy revelling, sweet
Rabbit, swan, pig's head.

Mia Elkes (9)
Broomgrove Junior School, Wivenhoe

Evacuation

Waiting for the train
Andy in arms and Lucy at my side
Oliver nudging me
Sally and Edward in the other arm
Fifteen layers for me, Janet.
'All aboard!' cries the conductor
In the train.

Alice Bell (7)
Broomgrove Junior School, Wivenhoe

Untitled

People falling through the air
Splash as they hit the sea
Some are swimming to the shore
But the sea is hungry for more

People on the boat
Scurrying, busy like ants
Racing to and fro
The Mary Rose is being swallowed.

A J Lawson (10)
Broomgrove Junior School, Wivenhoe

Evacuation

Waiting for a goodbye
With a green, soft, cuddly rabbit
With big, brown, soft shoes
Shaking from head to toe
When will I get there?
Where will I go?
Will it be very dark?
I want my mum!

Finnian Edwards (7)
Broomgrove Junior School, Wivenhoe

A Tudor Street

Stinky, smelly, suffocating
A Tudor street
Rowdy, cruel, scary
A Tudor street.

James Carmel (9)
Broomgrove Junior School, Wivenhoe

Henry VIII

Henry VIII had a big, fat tummy
And he thought things were really yummy.

Apart from veg - which he hated a lot,
Was it good for him? No, it was not!

He had six wives
And only one died.

He killed two more,
Blood galore!

One survived,
Henry died!
(Great for me!)

He had 14-16 courses a meal,
But I don't think he ate a lot of eel.

He ate swans and geese and porkies too,
I wonder if he ate a kangaroo?

Dancing and music was his fave,
But I don't think he was very brave.

200 servants worked for him
And their feelings were so very grim.

He had three children, Lizzie and Ed
And never forgetting the very best.

It's Bloody Mary, the best of all,
I wonder if she used a cannonball?

Bloody Mary matched her name,
'Cause killing Protestants was her game!

She locked her sister in the tower,
But while she was getting weaker by the hour.

Until she finally drop off dead,
I would have loved to chop off her mean little head!

Mollie McGill (10)
Brunswick House Primary School, Maidstone

Henry VIII

Henry VIII was very chubby,
For six unlucky women he was their hubby.

History books say he was divorced twice,
That's how we know he wasn't very nice.

Henry VIII beheaded two of his wives,
Sadly that meant they lost their lives.

He had two daughters and one son,
Mary, his eldest, wasn't any fun.

His eldest daughter was Bloody Mary,
She turned out to be very scary.

King Henry was so disgusting,
There turned out to be so much fussing.

King Henry had a very flat hat,
Although he was extremely fat.

King Henry was six feet two,
I wonder how he went to the loo.

Alexandra Bolou (10)
Brunswick House Primary School, Maidstone

Henry VIII

Henry the VIII had a big fat belly,
His tummy wobbled like a plate of jelly.

Henry the VIII had so many wives,
Most of them lost their lives.

He had such big, bulky thighs,
He ate all those pies.

In 1522 he went to war with the French,
I hear he got quite dirty when he slept in a trench.

He liked jousting and playing tennis
I heard he played tennis with his friend called Dennis.

Mitchell Maybourne (9)
Brunswick House Primary School, Maidstone

Henry VIII

Henry VIII was very chubby,
For six unlucky women he was their hubby.

History books say he was divorced twice,
That's how we know he wasn't very nice.

He had two daughters and one son,
Mary, his eldest wasn't any fun.

Henry has a daughter Princess Mary,
She turned out to be very scary.

Henry VIII had six wives,
I wondered if he spared their lives.

Two were divorced,
Heartbroken of course.

Two caught the sword,
They hurt the lord.

One died
And one survived.

Charlotte Crouch (9)
Brunswick House Primary School, Maidstone

Henry VIII

Henry the VIII had six beautiful wives,
We're extremely sad to report that two lost their lives.

He asked two of them for a divorce,
Especially Anne of Cleves who looked like a horse.

The only one to survive
Was lucky Catherine Parr, as Henry died.

He became king when he was only just eighteen,
He wanted a son and needed a queen.

As he got older he got horribly fat
And always behaved like a really spoilt brat!

Nicola Dear (9)
Brunswick House Primary School, Maidstone

Henry VIII

Henry VIII had six wives,
He seemed to like ruining their lives.

The only lucky one was little Catherine Parr,
She outlived her husband by far.

Henry explained, he's not fat
And liked to hit the black bat.

He only ruled for 38 years
And all that time he drank many beers.

When he was young he danced and sang
And married Catherine, she was his number one.

200 servants to see to his wishes,
He beheaded Anne for mixing with ugly witches.

In 1522 war was on with the French,
They may have had only a few pence.

Blood Mary was her name,
Killing Protestants was her ugly game.

Bobbi Jeffery (9)
Brunswick House Primary School, Maidstone

Henry VIII

Henry VIII was very chubby
For six unlucky women he was their hubby.

History books say he was divorced twice,
That's how we know he wasn't very nice.

He had two daughters and one son,
Mary, his eldest, wasn't any fun.

Bloody Mary turned out to be very scary.

Henry VIII had an enormous belly,
It is because he had too much jelly.

Sujata Gandhi (10)
Brunswick House Primary School, Maidstone

Henry VIII

Henry VIII was very chubby,
For six unlucky women he was their hubby.

History books say he was divorced twice,
That's how we know he wasn't very nice.

He had two daughters and a son,
His oldest, Mary, wasn't much fun.

Mary, Mary, is so scary,
Do you think she was hairy?

Liz, oh Liz, you think you were a whizz,
How could you think that, cos you went with a fizz.

Ed, poor Ed, you only ruled for six years,
When you caught a cold you dropped dead,
Eddie on the death bed.

Henry went to war with the French,
But I know he only sat on the bench.

Max Westall (9)
Brunswick House Primary School, Maidstone

Henry VIII

Henry the VIII was very chubby,
For six unlucky wives he was their hubby.

History books say he wasn't very nice,
That must be why he was divorced twice.

His eldest daughter, Princess Mary,
Turned out to be extremely scary.

Henry would even eat a tin,
His mouth was like a rubbish bin.

Henry loved to relax
Yet he never got out any of that ear wax.

Henry the VIII had a big, fat belly,
He must really like eating jelly.

Jake Hancock (10)
Brunswick House Primary School, Maidstone

Henry VIII

I'm Henry the VIII, I wear a hat,
Even though I'm very fat,
(Oh! I'm not that!)

Henry VIII had a big, fat tummy
And he thought things were very yummy,
Apart from veg which he hated,
This was what made him over weighted.
He had six wives and one died,
Killed two more, blood galore,
One survived, Henry died,
Great for me!

Hey, I'm not fat!

He had 14 to 16 courses a meal!
But don't think he liked eel.
He had dolphins in his belly,
Then it really wobbled like jelly!

Rebecca Lednor (9)
Brunswick House Primary School, Maidstone

Henry VIII

Henry VIII had six beautiful wives,
We're sad to report two lost their lives!

He asked two of them for a divorce,
Especially Anne of Cleves who looked like a horse!

The only one who survived
Was Catherine Parr as Henry died.

He became king when he was just eighteen,
He wanted a son and he needed a queen.

As he got older he got terribly fat
And always behaved like a really spoilt brat.

His fifth wife was Catherine Howard,
She never washed or ever showered!

Libby Gillett (9)
Brunswick House Primary School, Maidstone

Henry VIII

Henry VIII had an enormous belly
And it rumbled around like a bowl of jelly.

Henry VIII had too many wives,
If only they could have had nine lives.

He had such fat and bulky thighs
That's because he ate all those fatty pies.

In 1522 he went to war with the French,
I hear he used some men as his hench.

He liked to play a lot of tennis,
With his best mate called Dennis.

Henry VIII was six feet two,
I wonder how he got to the loo.

He enjoyed banquets and boiled meat,
I wonder how much he could eat.

Matthew Walker (9
Brunswick House Primary School, Maidstone

Henry VIII

I'm Henry VIII I wear a hat
I love to eat and I'm really fat.

I had six wives, now that's clear,
But Cath of Aragon, dear oh dear.

Married her for 24 years
Till the Spanish tried to invade,
Didn't give me an heir
So I divorced her
Then ate a jar of marmalade.

Anne Boleyn followed on,
She had a daughter instead of a son.

The best swordsman from France
Came over to England
To lend me a helping hand.

Emily Rye (9)
Brunswick House Primary School, Maidstone

Henry VIII

Henry the VIII I am,
I'm particularly fond of ham.

It goes to my belly,
Making it wobble like jelly.

I had six wives,
They had horrid lives,
I just got sick of glaring into their eyes.

I came to the throne at just 18 years old,
I rule my country with pots of shiny gold.

Books say I'm six feet two,
But is it really true?
I had to travel to my deathbed too soon,
Hey, guess what?
The time was twelve noon!

Liberty Jane Hardes (9)
Brunswick House Primary School, Maidstone

Henry VIII

Henry the VIII had a big fat belly,
When he sat down on the telly.

Henry VIII had so many wives,
So many wives that he ruined their lives.

He had such big and bulky thighs,
I think he ate too many pies.

In 1522 he went to war with the French,
Although I hear he only sat on the bench.

For entertainment he liked jousting and tennis,
Even though he was a big, big menace.

He liked banquets of roast and boiled meat,
Even though he had humungous, smelly feet.

Jeena Kotchakornkhonbut Light (9)
Brunswick House Primary School, Maidstone

Henry VIII

Podgy and chubby, fat Henry VIII,
I feel sorry for the things he ate.

Poor little piggy, shoved down his throat,
Henry was eating like a hungry goat!

Catherine of Aragon and Anne Boleyn
They were the first to marry him.

Then came Jane, the love of his life,
She didn't have long to be his wife.

She died in childbirth, (poor old thing),
After producing a son to please the king!

'Hey, that's not true about my size,
Neither is it about my wives!'

Kudzai-Nicole Chimwala (10)
Brunswick House Primary School, Maidstone

Henry VIII

Henry VIII was very chubby,
For six unlucky women he was their hubby.

History books say he was divorced twice,
That's how we know he wasn't very nice.

Henry VIII beheaded two of his wives,
Sadly that meant they lost their lives.

His eldest daughter was unfortunately, scary,
And her name was Bloody Mary.

King Henry had a very flat hat,
Although he was very fat.

King Henry was six feet two,
I wonder how he went to the loo.

Louis Ray (9)
Brunswick House Primary School, Maidstone

Henry VIII

Henry VIII had a big, fat belly,
He wobbled like a huge plate of grape jelly.

Henry VIII had so many pretty wives,
I'm surprised he had so many lives!

He had such big and bulging thighs,
I think he ate too many pies.

In 1522 he went to war with the horrible French,
I hear he got a bit dirty as he slept in a trench.

For entertainment he liked jousting and tennis,
But I heard he was quite a horrible menace.

He liked yummy banquets of roast and lovely boiled meat,
Although he had smelly feet!

Grace Brooks (10)
Brunswick House Primary School, Maidstone

Henry VIII

Henry VIII had a huge, fat belly,
I'm surprised he gets in his wellies!

Henry VIII had so many wives,
So many of them, ruined their lives.

He had such big and bulky thighs,
I think he ate too many pies!

In 1522 he went to war with the French,
I heard he got quite dirty when he slept in a trench.

For entertainment he liked jousting and tennis,
But I think he was a bit of a menace.

He likes proud banquets of roast and boiled meat,
But I think he liked them nice and sweet.

Poppy Bishop (9)
Brunswick House Primary School, Maidstone

Henry VIII

Henry VIII I really am,
I'm particularly fond of yummy ham.

It goes to my humungous belly,
Making it wobble like orange jelly.

I had six wives, they had horrible lives,
I just got sick of glaring into their frightful eyes.

I came to the throne at 18 years old,
I rule my huge country with pots of gold.

Thick books say I am six feet two,
But is that really true?

I went to my deathbed way too soon,
Guess what - the time was noon!

Natasha Longley (10)
Brunswick House Primary School, Maidstone

Henry VIII

Henry VIII had an enormous belly,
Sometimes it wobbled like strawberry jelly.

Henry VII had so many wives,
Most of them died and lost their lives.

He had such big and bulky thighs
That's because he ate loads and loads of pies.

In 1522 he went to war with the French,
I hear he got quite dirty when he slept in a trench.

Kimberley Bennett (10)
Brunswick House Primary School, Maidstone

Henry VIII

Henry the VIII had six beautiful wives,
Sad to report two lost their lives.

He asked two of them for a divorce,
Especially Anne of Cleves who looked like a horse.

He became king when he was just eighteen,
He wanted a son and badly needed a queen.

As he got older he got horribly fat
And always behaved like a spoilt brat.

Holly Palmer (9)
Brunswick House Primary School, Maidstone

Henry VIII

Henry VIII had six horrid wives,
We're sad to report two lost their lives.

As he got older he got fat
And always behaved like a spoilt brat.

He became king when he was just eighteen,
He wanted a son and needed a queen.

He asked two of them for a divorce,
Especially Anne of Cleves who looked like a horse!

Ben Brown (9)
Brunswick House Primary School, Maidstone

Aztecs

A ztecs are different
Z ooming to catch their prey
T rying to find a place to put a town
E ager to find an eagle eating a serpent
C utting their heads off
S mashing history.

Zilan Hamzaogullari (9)
Claremont Primary School, Tunbridge Wells

Perilous People Through Time

Up in Asia, the Chinese ruled,
They invented martial arts which are rather cool.
Their dynasties included Zhou and Han
And they believed the emperor had to be a man.

Down in Africa, the Egyptians had the throne,
They did a lot of mummifying, which is well known.
Their pyramids were higher than the tallest tree,
And the River Nile trailed through this country.

Centred in the sea is Greece, (a lovely place),
In 750BC they had the first Olympic race.
They used bronze and iron weapons to fight all their wars.
It was so long ago that no one knows the cause.

Nearby, in Italy, the Romans were having fun,
Dipped in the Mediterranean with lots of boiling sun.
In the Coliseum they had many violent fights,
They also made mosaics which were awe-inspiring sights.

Up north sailed the Vikings in their elongated ships,
They travelled around Europe on a discovery trip.
They ate loads of fish that meant they would have been quite clever,
It that was true their Empire should have lasted forever.

Down south-west the Aztecs were in power,
The eagle and snake showed them where to build their tower.
Riding around in boats because they had lots of rivers,
They sacrificed everything, which will probably make you shiver.

And then of course, there's us, who have all these things,
Houses, churches, roads and telephones that ring.
Planes and bombs instead of spears to fight our wars,
We are still determined to protect our shores.

George FitzGerald (8)
Claremont Primary School, Tunbridge Wells

The Vikings

One stormy night something gave me a fright,
The Vikings, the Vikings!
In longboats they came,
Creeping down lane by lane.
Bloodthirsty lot the Vikings were,
Scarlet red beards like burning fire, each Viking had one.
Finding riches beyond the land,
Terrorising people, taking out of their hands.
House by house they stole from,
Scaring and killing whatever came in their way!
Home they went and back again,
Looking for more every time.
So just travel back in rhyme!

Ellie Brown (8)
Claremont Primary School, Tunbridge Wells

Chimney Sweep

My master sings a song
To help him get along
He pushes my foot
As I sneeze on the soot
I was feeling ill
And there are no pills
Oh, we hate the Victorian times
Now listen to these lines
As I begin to choke
A whopping great bloke
Pulls me down from Hell
Oh, I hate the Victorian times.

Lauren Grant & Hannah Godsmark (8)
Claremont Primary School, Tunbridge Wells

World War Two

W hile the bombs dropped on the towns.
O ld people hid underground.
R ound and round went the planes,
L ong, long ways went the trains.
D inner was rationed for all,

W hen will we eat, if ever at all?
A dolph Hitler is his name,
R uling Europe was his aim.

T wo by two children got on the trains, some never seen again.
W ill England win this horrid war?
O h God please make things the way they were before.

Grace Forbes (8)
Claremont Primary School, Tunbridge Wells

Angry Aztecs

They stab your hearts like they're jam tarts.
They are sore after war.
Blood drips from their hearts like darts.
Their pyramids are big,
Like overgrown pigs.
They think about their gods
Hunting souls.
Their art is so good,
It's like painted wood.

Ruben Dascombe & Harry Child (8)
Claremont Primary School, Tunbridge Wells

Cleopatra

C leopatra the royal queen
L ean and mean
E xtreme killer
O nly bathes in milk
P erfect lining, dress of silk
A fter that she wears a fake beard
T hough her face is smeared with grace
R eminds her of her son
A fter that, bye-bye, she dies in a pit of lies!

Emma Shepherd (10)
Claremont Primary School, Tunbridge Wells

Is WW2 The Place For You?

Is World War Two the place for you?
No, no way,
They're dropping bombs every day.
The Jerries are Britain's enemy,
They're dropping bombs so fiercely.
Go. Run, shoo, flee;
Run away and soon you'll see!

Emily Ballara & Isobel Poland (9)
Claremont Primary School, Tunbridge Wells

Dinosaur Rampage

In the sky pterodactyls fly
On the ground diplodocus stomps
But closing in is a ginormous T-Rex roaring an almighty roar
But diplodocus slams him with his thrashing tail
So T-rex swipes but misses
And pterodactyl throws a massive peck in his staring eye
To blind him
So that was the end of T-rex!

Matthew Dubery (7)
Claremont Primary School, Tunbridge Wells

Family Tree

Spread put on the table
Lay parchment crumpled and crisp,
With corners bending inward
And writing fine as silk.
The names lay scattered on the page,
With branches everywhere
And there my name lay, nice and new
To be discovered by someone like you.

Lily Montague (10)
Claremont Primary School, Tunbridge Wells

Blast To The Past

Dreadful dinosaurs

Stomp, crash, boom, smash
A natural, pure cacophony,
Dinosaurs, could it be?

The grave Great Fire of London

The year was 1666,
A truly dreadful night,
A baker's shop in Pudding Lane
Was fondly set alight.

Divorced, beheaded, died, divorced, beheaded, survived

Atop the tower
Young Anne awaits,
To seal her dreadful, doomed fate,
Soon to be followed by two more wives,
She lays her head down on the block,
The executioner's axe goes *chop!*

Now we reach the final straw, we have invented even more.

Now we live our daily lives
Filing cabinets open wide,
There's so much more that's entered our world
Throughout the years
And so much more to come, like -

Coke powered cars and much, much more,
When you open up the floor,
Waterslides got to your back door
Hover jets and rocket powered underpants
That fly you to the moon,

Bonnie Vincent & Holly Cummings (10)
Claremont Primary School, Tunbridge Wells

Boudicca's Revolt

Long hair flying
Shiny sword waving
Face all scary
Boudicca!

Glinting armour
Eagle-fronted shields
Marching down the hill
Romans!

Bare-chested bodies
Painted faces
Shouting loudly
Celts!

Jorja Cocks (7)
Crowstone Preparatory School, Westcliff-on-Sea

Boudicca's Revolt

Arrows flying in the air
Helmets shining in the sun
I can feel my heart beating
People being sick
Angry face on Boudicca
Horses sinking in the mud
Soldiers shouting
Soldiers screaming
Horses dying in the mud!

Kitty Norris (7)
Crowstone Preparatory School, Westcliff-on-Sea

Boudicca's Battle

Sharp swords clashing
Big shields bashing
Houses burning
Chariot wheels turning
Horses galloping
In the sun
Shouts so loud
The battle's just begun!

Amber Clark (7)
Crowstone Preparatory School, Westcliff-on-Sea

Vicious Vikings

Snort, lump and scrawny are the words Vikings used,
How do you keep them amused?
Viking shoes were often blue,
As well as red too.

Vikings did not use pens,
But did they build dens?
Vikings made wool from sheep,
We can't believe they did not weep.

Vikings kept bees for honey,
But that's not very funny!
Vikings cooked meat in a pit,
I wonder if they used a tool kit.

Vikings believed that the world was flat,
Their clothes are probably made from tat,
They told myths about trolls
And we bet they acted it out with dolls.

Thank you very much for listening,
But sadly now the Vikings are missing.

Ellie Stoneman, Lucy Cole & Milla Hanson
Dymchurch Primary School, Dymchurch

Can You Spell Dinosaurs

D is for dinosaurs that are now extinct,
I is for ignorant dinos, just don't think.
N is for nice, close but not quiet,
O is for option, hunt or bite!
S is for sometimes they hunt or play,
A is for angry night and day.
U is for ugly, not all, but some,
R is for rude, some are quiet dumb.
S is for sky where pterodactyls fly.

Tommy Clements (10), Acey Little & Matthew Hurst
Dymchurch Primary School, Dymchurch

My Poem About World War II

This is my poem about World War II
Rumours about Hitler being good were not true,
Winston Churchill was the great man,
He always looked very smart and grand.

The war only went on for a few years,
Though it made a lot of good people burst into tears,
Hitler made men go to war,
But when they came back home they felt very sore.

Children were sent away on trains,
To keep them away from all the pain,
You hear them shout and you hear them scream,
But now they regret saying, 'Mum, you're really mean!'

Some sadly didn't come home,
But the lucky ones were glad they were no longer alone,
Winston Churchill's good deeds were done,
Because World War II was over and England had won.

Tegan Hooper (11)
Dymchurch Primary School, Dymchurch

War

The bomb smoke kissed my cheeks,
As they spread across the area.
The vibrations of the helicopters above,
It was raining bombs
As the soldiers made a run for it.
I could see the tired soldiers
Huddled together,
I could hear
The rat-a-tat-tat of machine gun fire.
The roar of planes
Flying overhead,
I could smell the gunpowder
As the bullets were fired.
The poppies nodded their red heads
As the soldiers fought for their lives.

Lara Jones-Wise (9)
Great Clacton CE (VA) Junior School, Great Clacton

Life In The War

Men lying dead on the ground,
Blood running down their faces,
People running scared, people getting to safety.
Children injured and screaming.
Bullets escorting people to the ground,
My teammates whispering their last words, goodbye,
Before falling to the ground,
Dead soldiers covered in ash.
God whispered in my ear before I died,
Helicopters getting injured men out.
But we won the war.
Poppies are where soldiers once laid.

Pippa Saunders (9)
Great Clacton CE (VA) Junior School, Great Clacton

Atrocious World War

Countries at war, oh so fierce,
The soldiers' friends dying in front of their eyes.
Oh what a horrible sight.
Dark green grenades with their wobbling fat bodies
Zooming across the sky.
The enormous rats in the trenches are giant horses
Galloping to and fro.
Inky bombs whizzing through the air,
The smells of dead bodies odouring the war grounds.
The smell of rosy red fire coming from the burning house.
The sound of the enemies' air rifles is like a million lions
Roaring at the same time.
The wind from the helicopters is like a hurricane
Trying to knock me over,
The sound from the Spitfires is like a storm
That will go on for a hundred years.

The soldiers are a pack of fearless cheetahs
Waiting to pounce on their prey.
The smoke that comes from the gigantic bombs
Is a massive rain cloud covering the Earth.

Savannah Partridge (9)
Great Clacton CE (VA) Junior School, Great Clacton

World At War

Sad soldiers died together
I can smell the black smoke from fires caused by bombs
I can hear explosions from the black, cloudy sky
I can feel the sadness
From the dying soldiers around me.

Harry Chung (9)
Great Clacton CE (VA) Junior School, Great Clacton

Terrifying War

Bright bullets exploding
Colourful, like a rainbow
Smoke spreading through the fresh air
People flying to the ground
A flock of helicopters trying to shove me over
The peaceful dead lay on the floor
Hear the bullets fly above my head
You can hear the people screaming for safety
The sky is ink

The blood sails around
The rat-a-tat of the bullets
Smoke from the impact of a bomb hit
Sadness spreading around
The squidgy mud under their feet
You can smell the smoke in the air
People cry all around.

Michelle Thomas (9)
Great Clacton CE (VA) Junior School, Great Clacton

World At War

Brave soldiers looking scared and tough,
Soldiers are praying for their lives.
The smell of thick black smoke from the impact of a bomb.
The gunpowder stank like rotten cheese.
All you could hear were tired, screaming, dying soldiers,
Banging guns firing every second.
The wind sang an emotional song to the soldiers
As they sadly passed away.
A bullet kissed my heart and took me to the wet ground,
The ash wiped me out before I could run.
Sadly you have to say goodbye and watch them float to Heaven.
God whispered to my ear and said, 'Don't give up.'
God floated beside me all the way.
The army soldiers are most exhausted people right now.
The bright red poppies bowed their heads
And softly said, 'Just keep going.'

Ben Vickers (10)
Great Clacton CE (VA) Junior School, Great Clacton

Poppies And Battle

A bomb on the floor going to bang!
All I can hear is tired, screaming babies
Almost like a big lake of tears kissing my face
As my teammate escorted me to
The rubble on the dusty ground
Then my teammate whispered to me his last words
'Goodbye.'
And that was it,
But the good thing was I knew God was right beside me
The whole way through my journey!

Then, *bang!* right in my heart,
Dynamite struck and I sadly passed away
But I also knew that the poppies were bowing their heads
In respect for me and my teammates!
Thank you poppies and that was it.

Jessica Chirgwin (9)
Great Clacton CE (VA) Junior School, Great Clacton

At War

Smell the drifting smoke from the burning houses,
Sadness all around,
Terrified people shouting for safety,
People crying in the distance,
The roaring sound of grenades
And RPGs in the air.
In the dark, scary bunkers,
Germans setting up their guns.
Terrified, trembling.
Grass swaying side to side,
People's guns firing quickly,
Fearless army tanks firing
Bombs that chatter in the air.

Kai Ridgeon (9)
Great Clacton CE (VA) Junior School, Great Clacton

World At War

The bomb's smoke kissed my cheeks,
As they spread the area,
You can see the gunships moving out.
While you are feeling sad your team mates are feeling sad too.
The rat-a-tat of the machine gun fire,
I can see the mortar strike coming down at me.
I can smell the impact of the bombs.
The grenades come down ferociously,
As mean as a volcano
As the soldiers make a run for it.
I can see the sensory gun killing the soldiers.
The poppies showed their red heads
As the soldiers fight for their lives.

Jack Lingwood (9)
Great Clacton CE (VA) Junior School, Great Clacton

On The Battlefield

Mighty helicopters flying rapidly
Like flocks of black crows,
The drifting smoke fills the disgusting, rank air around them.
Sharp, speedy, flying from every direction
Travelling at the speed of light.
Afraid, terrified, petrified, scared soldiers,
Fighting for their lives and for their country.
Rat-a-tat, the machine gun spits out all of its bullets at once.
It was almost as if you could smell the fear
Of all the soldiers in the army.
Bright bombs exploding,
Like fireworks on New Year's Day.

Thomas Cooper (9)
Great Clacton CE (VA) Junior School, Great Clacton

Poppies And The Battle

People with no homes or family,
Evil and good hearts.
The gunpowder smells like a bomb just exploded,
You could hear the soldiers screaming in pain.
The thought of my family enters my head,
The wind sings an emotional song to the soldiers
As they pass away.
God whispers to the soldiers
As they walk along their dark, lonely way.
The rain kissed my face while the bombs escorted me to the ground.
The poppies nodded their red heads
Showing their respect for the soldiers.

Millie Dellar (9)
Great Clacton CE (VA) Junior School, Great Clacton

War

Abandoned people with their legs sticking out of a hole
Covered with stinky mud.
You could see the bombs smashing rapidly at my face
As they fell,
I spluttered and choked
As a bullet flew into my chest.
People heard helicopters flying noisily over their heads.
They felt people pushing past them
To get to the family they had left.
I would win a medal for bravery,
But after that I fell to the ground.
The poppies nodded their red heads in respect.

Emma Garn (10)
Great Clacton CE (VA) Junior School, Great Clacton

World At War

The grass shivers slightly as the wind blows,
When you're on there's no way out!
The wind whistles loudly past my ears,
Good and evil hearts go into this war.
Some make it, some don't.
As the blood from my forehead kisses my lips
I run for the victim, but bang!
Suddenly I fall to the muddy, wet ground.
That's why the little red heads bow,
For the people who died in war!
And so do I.

Thomas England (9)
Great Clacton CE (VA) Junior School, Great Clacton

Woeful War

The dead all scattered around me,
Bright bombs exploding in thin air,
The unfortunate moans of the soldiers,
The bullets are F1 race cars
Zooming round the track,
My injured friend dying before my eyes.

It really is a horrible sight,
I feel my heart cracking in two,
Mighty helicopters flying rapidly
Like giant storks.

William Goody (9)
Great Clacton CE (VA) Junior School, Great Clacton

World War One

Soldiers charging at each other,
Tanks throwing bombs
You can hear the deafening noise.
Exploding in the background
Bright bombs,
Booming, exploding in the thin air.

Peaceful now
The enemy retreats to base.
Quiet, as the people walk around
And the helicopters look for enemies.

Daniel Foster (9)
Great Clacton CE (VA) Junior School, Great Clacton

Helicopter Terror

The dead in wastelands.
Helicopter whizzing past soldiers with a rumble.
Injured soldiers filling up the shotguns
Ready to go to battle.
The black, inky bonfire coming from houses.
The wretched smell of blood.
The gunshots all around.

The ground blasting beneath their feet.
People and children in danger.
Mums and dads rushing to be saved.

Nathan Mills (9)
Great Clacton CE (VA) Junior School, Great Clacton

The War That Ended With A Bang

Bullets hitting the huddled group and the ground,
The smell was nothing like home,
You can hear a missile coming straight for you!
You feel upset to hear your friend has been shot.
As the gunshot wind blows away, they ambush you.
We were happy to think the war was over, but it wasn't.
Yet they struck a bomb and wiped out all but me.
The war was supposed to end,
As I pulled the trigger it pushed me back to the ground,
Eventually we won the war and I got back to my worried family.

Ian Stainer (9)
Great Clacton CE (VA) Junior School, Great Clacton

At War

Bullets zoom past all over the place,
It sounds like they whistle as they go.
Bombs soaring through the air
And blowing up with a thunderous boom.

The pressure of the helicopters pushing on the soldiers
Like huge boulders landing on them.
Lots of innocent people lying on the ground,
Like trees that have been brutally cut down.
The blades of the helicopters are blasting to my ears.

Michael England (9)
Great Clacton CE (VA) Junior School, Great Clacton

War

I can feel the bomb's vibrations through my feet
I can feel the rocks kissing my cheeks
I can feel the rocks raining all around me
Dust goes into my tired eyes
I am sad to hear my friends getting shot
And I think I am going to die.

William Shuttleworth (9)
Great Clacton CE (VA) Junior School, Great Clacton

War

The soldiers feel like they're not alive,
Hearts beating fast like they're about to explode.
Bombs exploding frighteningly
Bullets zooming towards the noisy helicopters up above.
Black smoke hanging in the air
Like a big rain cloud.
Thick smog everywhere,
Like you don't know where you are.
Dead soldiers scattered around the dirty, muddy field.

Serena Berry (9)
Great Clacton CE (VA) Junior School, Great Clacton

World At War

Bright bombs exploding in thin air
Dead bodies resting in the background
Far, far away
Bombs exploding like tornadoes
Gigantic helicopters making noises like a motorbike
Enormous helicopters trying to push teams to the floor
Huge helicopters trying to knock them over
People shouting for help
But all they could hear was a baby crying.

Charlie Riley (9)
Great Clacton CE (VA) Junior School, Great Clacton

World In Pain

Smell the smoking houses, it fills their nostrils,
The stench of the smog makes them cough and choke.
The horrendous smoke is as foul as someone smoking a cigarette,
Soldiers feeling like their empty hearts are being shot down
Screaming in their ears.

Soldiers lying dead like sleeping lions
At a children's party and lying peacefully
Still as ice cubes.

Connor Smith (9)
Great Clacton CE (VA) Junior School, Great Clacton

War

Soldiers crying tears of death
The blood of a soldier hits my cheek
As he got shot to the ground.
The earth kissed my cheek and whispered in my ear,
'Don't give up!' as I hit the ground, face first.
The smell of the bombs stinks like rotten food,
Tired, sick soldiers injured on the ground.
The mud in my toes squishy and sickly,
The poppies in the wind bow in respect for the soldiers.

Kiera Gubbins (10)
Great Clacton CE (VA) Junior School, Great Clacton

Terrified

Tanks clunking over mountains getting ready to eat people up,
Gunshots booming.
Grenades blowing up, lighting up the sky,
Innocent people getting shot into the air
Like kangaroos bouncing back to the ground,
Soldiers dead from the fighting,
It was like a graveyard,
Eerie and spooky,
The soldiers scared and sad.

Ryan Everett (9)
Great Clacton CE (VA) Junior School, Great Clacton

Life In The Army

Tired soldiers huddling together,
The sound of bombs blowing and guns firing.
Loads of people screaming,
Like sharks hunting for their prey,
Vibrations from the helicopters circling around me,
The blood dripping from my forehead,
Kissing my dry lips.

Poppies now grow where soldiers once laid.

Leah Perkins (10)
Great Clacton CE (VA) Junior School, Great Clacton

Pain

The dead lying peacefully in the middle of the wastelands
Helicopters wobbling over soldiers
Their fat bodies trying to knock soldiers over,
Tanks shooting at the opposition.

Black, inky bomb fire in the enemy fields
People yelling, crying like lions roaring,
All of the children are leaving the country
It is war.

Adam Hemmings (9)
Great Clacton CE (VA) Junior School, Great Clacton

The Crazy War

Flame-throwers are spitting fire at the enemies,
So quickly bright bombs exploding in the air.
Helicopters cruising past slowly,
So gentle.
The enemies scatter everywhere.
Inky black smoke,
Machine gun bullets scatter all over the land.
Men blow up the enemy helpers.

Callum Earl (9)
Great Clacton CE (VA) Junior School, Great Clacton

Life At War

Bombs brighten up the sky,
Lots of soldiers huddling together
People screaming all over the place,
Bombs exploding in the distance.
The rat-a-tat of the guns scared me
Bullets flew over my head as fast as lightning.
The red poppies looked at me in respect
As I fall to the ground.

Alexander Ktori (9)
Great Clacton CE (VA) Junior School, Great Clacton

Soldiers At War

The giant helicopter was whooshing
And my boiling, red brain is ready to explode.

Bullets coming down to my shelter
Like shooting stars
Getting their revenge back on us.

Nowhere to hide,
Noise like thunder all around.

Ryan Moore (9)
Great Clacton CE (VA) Junior School, Great Clacton

War

Tired soldiers
Huddled together on the cold winter ground
The tired soldiers
Trying to find water and food
But nothing, just snow around
And bombs falling from the sky every second

The flower follows you wherever you lay your sweet head.

Shanae Noel (9)
Great Clacton CE (VA) Junior School, Great Clacton

The Disgusting, Despicable War

Guns zooming above soldiers' heads,
Black, inky bombs bursting in the floor
Like a piece of wood banging on a bit of metal.

Helicopters roaring like tigers having a fight.
The cold breeze on the soldiers' bodies,
Helicopters wobbling their fat bodies
Try to knock the soldiers over.

Casey Haynes (10)
Great Clacton CE (VA) Junior School, Great Clacton

The Sad War

Dark, heavy smoke in the distance
Rolling nearer and nearer like a giant wave

Helicopters flying overhead
Like birds of prey watching.

Waiting, land, scared, lonely.

When will this unhappiness end?

Adriana Cotirlea (9)
Great Clacton CE (VA) Junior School, Great Clacton

The War Poem

Tired soldiers huddle together
You can hear exploding bombs in the distance
Warm blood running down my body
People pushing past to get to their family
The poppy nodded her head
As it lay where once was a war.

Chloe Towler (9)
Great Clacton CE (VA) Junior School, Great Clacton

The Bad War

The enormous helicopter flying overhead
The wind swirling around like a tornado
Soldiers tamping and sliding through the long grass
Muggy and hot
Like someone had opened the oven
Gasping for air.

Teejay Apps (9)
Great Clacton CE (VA) Junior School, Great Clacton

A Feisty War

Smell the blazing smoke that fills the inky black sky,
Like a giant rain cloud ready to explode,
Helicopters so quick they felt like they were anxious,
Tornado heading for a great big family trying to get away
From the horrible horror movie
Waiting to be saved.

Jenna-Rose Baker (9)
Great Clacton CE (VA) Junior School, Great Clacton

Back In Rhyme

In the streets of Tudor London,
Where Queen Elizabeth the First ruled,
A genius, named William Shakespeare
Sat with a quill in hand as his brain cooled

His mind was racing around and around
'I must get this right, confound!'
Wax burned on the candle,
Moths were drawn to the light
Shakespeare's got writer's block, what blight!

The next morning dawned
Roses begun to thorn
William's play was written
His adoring future audience will be smitten

Royalty approaches
In horse-driven coaches
A play for the ages
Queen Elizabeth the First rages

Richard III, the play of course!
The actor cried,
'A horse, my kingdom for a horse!'
That sentence will be famous nationwide.

Saul Levene (11)
Ilford Jewish Primary School, Ilford

As I Went Back In Tudor Times

As I went back in Tudor Time
The clock striking one
I smelt the maid cooking for
Henry VIII, a hot cross bun.

As I went back in Tudor Time
The clock striking two
I heard a man screaming
Because he saw Anne being executed.

As I went back in Tudor Time
The clock striking three
I saw a man walking
With his very ill children.

As I went back in Tudor Time
The clock striking four
I can smell everyone's disgusting teeth
Which were black and crusty.

Now never go back in Tudor time
Henry VIII may catch you
So beware and make sure
You're safe or you'll be beheaded.

Ellie Grant (10)
Ilford Jewish Primary School, Ilford

The Titanic

I feel the sadness and tears,
I hear the cries of frightened children,

I can feel the freezing water,
I can taste the salty ocean,
I can hear the iceberg cracking,

I can touch the icy water,
I can feel the water on my neck,
I can feel the tension all around me.

Miss T Dias (9)
Ilford Jewish Primary School, Ilford

WWII

There I was face
To face with
The man himself
Adolf Hitler
Was his name
Now I have to tell
You, this coming
From an
Englishman
That he
Was no friend
Of mine or anyone
Else for that
Matter
He said
Something to do
With a plan for conquering
The world.
Between you
And me, I
Wasn't really listening
Either.
I've also
Been extremely angry
With these Germans lately
Because, well one
Of my
Friends
Got
Shot, it was
A tremendous day for
Me anyway
I shot one
Of the main
Commanders of
The Japanese
Army
I can
Tell you the
UK were pretty
Pleased with me!

And that
My friends is
What happened to me
In WWII!

Dalia Sweiry (11)
Ilford Jewish Primary School, Ilford

Bang Goes The Cowboy

I heard the words shoot out of his mouth,
I saw someone scream down south,
I watched them die, it looked bad,
It's worse for them, oh what a poor lad.

I shot a cowboy in the head,
He laid down, definitely dead,
The cowboy had brown, short hair,
I felt bad, It wasn't fair.

I saw a cactus, long and green,
Saw another cowboy, he looked mean,
He shot a bullet in the air,
He looked deadly, I didn't care.

His horse was white, white and skinny,
Its name was - yes, I think it was Binny,
He shot me with a dart,
It was too painful, I was falling apart.

I felt really weak and frail,
I was dying, I looked very pale,
A guy gave me an antidote,
He stuck it in my throat.

I swallowed it. Swallowed it hard,
I think I was definitely scarred,
I fled away, out of sight,
Why did I have to fight?

I laid down, I went to sleep,
I couldn't so I counted sheep.

Daniel Oster (9)
Ilford Jewish Primary School, Ilford

World War II

I went back in time
And I was really scared,
I nearly forgot that my foot had not been repaired,
So I couldn't run and I couldn't hide,
The only thing I could do was ride.

I heard a lot of things,
I heard the *boom* of the bombs in the night sky,
I also heard the hammering of the nasty guns,
I didn't like it in WWII,
Not at all.

I went back in time
And I was really scared,
I nearly forgot that my foot had not been repaired,
So I couldn't run and I couldn't hide,
The only thing I could do was ride.

I saw a lot of things,
I saw the soldiers all huddling together,
Just to keep warm,
Also I saw the brave soldiers battling
For their country, their children and their wives,
I didn't like it in WWII,
Not at all.

I went back in time
And I was really scared,
I nearly forgot that my foot had not been repaired,
So I couldn't run and I couldn't hide,
The only thing I could do was ride.

I felt a lot of things,
I felt the wet, squelchy mud on my feet,
Which wasn't very nice,
Also I felt the drizzle if rain down my neck,
I didn't like it in WWII,
Not at all.

I went back in time
And I was really scared,
I nearly forgot that my foot had not been repaired,
So I couldn't run and I couldn't hide,
The only thing I could do was ride.

Abbie Oster (9)
Ilford Jewish Primary School, Ilford

Dinosaurs

As I went back in time
The clock striking one,
I saw a dinosaur chewing
A lump of strawberry bubblegum.

As I went back in time
The clock striking two,
I heard a dinosaur roaring
Whilst the wind blew.

As I went back in time
The clock striking three,
I saw a dinosaur running
Running after me.

As I went back in time
The clock striking four,
I spied a huge dinosaur
Smash through my door.

As I went back in time
The clock striking five,
I saw a massive dinosaur
Smashing through a beehive.

Matilda Livngstone (9)
Ilford Jewish Primary School, Ilford

Henry VIII

In the glorious age of the Tudors
There was one main king
His name was Henry 8th
And he had no bling

Henry had red hair, a frizzy beard
And he loved to eat
His favourite thing to devour
Was lovely, fresh meat

Henry had six wives
They all hated him
None of them spent
More than ten years with him

Henry died at 56
From an infected leg
He laid on his deathbed
Ready to beg.

Jack Chevin (9)
Ilford Jewish Primary School, Ilford

Henry Said

(Inspired by Michael Rosen's 'Rodge Said')

Henry said,
'Wives, they're annoying always.
Are you giving birth to a girl or something?'
And she says,
'Yes, I'm giving birth, have you got a problem?'
So Henry said, 'Yes, I want a boy.'
And she says,
'That's not very nice.'
'But if I said, do you want a divorce?'
She said, 'You can't get divorced in this country.'
'But I say I make the rules round here and I say you can.
Wives, they're annoying always!'
Henry said.

Abigail Fay Preston (9)
Ilford Jewish Primary School, Ilford

Rotten Romans

Once in the Roman days
No one was very nice
People who I saw were robbers
In the Roman days they were like snaky mice

In the Roman army
People were so loud
Everyone had to go into
A colossal crowd

Every day in the Roman streets
There was business on the floor
It was so smelly
Lots of people were very poor

Where the shops were
You couldn't buy one thing of each
Lots of Roman days
People don't like to teach.

Isabella Francis Cope (9)
Ilford Jewish Primary School, Ilford

The War

I walked out onto the field and I heard a terrible thud
And I could see I was covered in blood.

I thought it was the end
And I was never going to mend.

I could smell and taste thick smoke
And I thought I was going to choke.

But then someone came near
And I had a tear trickling down my face.

An ambulance came to drain away the horrendous pain
Then I was put on a plane.

Thank God I am out of this dreadful war
But I have been left very sore.

Jasmine Cohen (10)
Ilford Jewish Primary School, Ilford

Egyptian Said

The Egyptian said,
'Pharaoh - he want is all ways,
You're sitting down instead of doing your work or something
And he says,
'Get up, make my statue now!'

So you say, 'Yes Pharaoh.
And he says,
'Make sure it looks like me!'

But if you say, 'Do I have to?'
He says,
'You should or you will be buried
Under the Sphinx.'
Thanks you very much.

'Pharaoh, he gets you all ways,'
Egyptians said.

Aimee Nossek (10)
Ilford Jewish Primary School, Ilford

The Great Fire Of London

I can see the big flames in the air,
I can smell the fire - why do I care?
I can hear the shouting all around,
I can feel the tower falling,
I can go and try to get help,
The sky can touch the flames,
I can call someone,
Because they're all dying, they're crying.

The tower's falling, it's very sad,
I don't like it because there's loads of fire.
People all around, they're trying to help,
There is loads of fire.
Why is everyone going to cry?
I need someone because of the fire.
I want it to stop.

Amber Tassie (9)
Ilford Jewish Primary School, Ilford

Awful Egyptians

Pharaoh, Pharaoh, why are you like this?
I see people dying for you
Pharaoh, Pharaoh, why are you like this?
I see people struggling for you

Pharaoh, Pharaoh, why are you like this?
I hear women crying for you
Pharaoh, Pharaoh, why are you like this?
I hear people sacrificing for you

Pharaoh, Pharaoh, why are you like this?
I feel people's pain for you
Pharaoh, Pharaoh, why are you like this?
I feel the slaves getting whipped for you

Pharaoh, Pharaoh,
Why are you like this?

Ellie Partridge (9)
Ilford Jewish Primary School, Ilford

Titanic

It's like a tipping back ride,
The water, it freezes my body,
He swims with me, by my side.

He tells me, 'Don't worry,
We'll do this together,
We really must hurry.'

I hear all the screaming,
It's scaring me much,
The boat won't stop leaning.

I'm starting to sink,
So as we sink he says,
'Hold on . . .'

Keeleigh Zaydner (9)
Ilford Jewish Primary School, Ilford

King Henry VIII

I am hungry
I'm going to
Play tennis with
My servant, even
Though I'm certain
I'll win!
Ooh, what is
That I smell?
Food, can't wait
To eat that!
Right, back to tennis.

Phoebe Myers (10)
Ilford Jewish Primary School, Ilford

Great Fire Of London

I can see great flames pop and feel hot burning and smoke
I can taste hot cinders and smoke
I can hear flames burning houses down
And shops as I watch people crying and screaming
In the dark, as their house are burnt at night
I can hear choking therefore I can't hear myself think.

Jordana Baron (9)
Ilford Jewish Primary School, Ilford

Being An Evacuee

Us children are saying goodbye to our mum,
I've never been away from her for that long before.
I'll have my brothers and sister to keep me company,
On the train I whimper, my sister says it will be fine.
I know she is scared, all of us are.
We arrive at the train station,
It's been six months since we've seen each other.

Now we can go home,
I see my mum and give her a big *hug!*

Ellyn Dever (10)
Joy Lane Primary School, Whitstable

Victorians

(Queen Victoria's reign lasted from 20th June 1837 until her death on 22nd January 1901)

Britain built a huge empire during the Victorian period. In 1837 most people lived in villages and worked on the land; by 1901, most lived in towns and worked in offices, shops and factories.

Britain became the most powerful and richest country in the world, with the largest empire that had ever existed, ruling a quarter of the world's population.

The number of people living in Britain more than doubled from 16 million to 37 million, causing a huge demand for food, clothes and housing.

There were no painkillers nor anaesthesia for the Victorians - operations went on for hours with patients in excruciating agony.

The police force was created during the Victorian period by Sir Robert Peel (hence the nickname 'Bobbies').

To control insects, many people kept a hedgehog in the basement. It curled up and slept in the day, but roamed around the dark kitchen at night eating cockroaches and other insects.

Children were often forced to work. Many were used as cheap labour in factories, or as chimney sweeps. The work was dangerous and painful. Some boys got stuck and died of suffocation.

Henry VIII & Tudors

(Henry's reign 28th June 1491 – 28th January 1547 Tudor dynasty from 1485 until 1603)

The first Tudor king was Henry VII. He became king after the Battle of Bosworth Field, which ended the Wars of the Roses.

Henry VIII is probably the most well known of the Tudor monarchs. He was a very selfish person and by the end of his life everyone was afraid of him, mainly because of his ruthless behaviour toward anyone who didn't agree with him.

In 1534, Henry VIII broke away from the Catholic Church and proclaimed himself head of the Church of England. Henry sold off the land and riches of the church to dukes, barons and other noblemen.

Contrary to popular opinion, Henry VIII had many children. Unfortunately it was very common in Tudor times for them to die very young. Only three survived beyond childhood.

An average person drank about 8 pints of 'weak beer' a day. It had very little alcohol in it, and even children drank it. It was safer than the water available at the time.

The ending of the marriages of King Henry VIII can be remembered by the following rhyme:
'Divorced, beheaded, died divorced, beheaded, survived'.

Boudicca

Died between 60 and 62 AD

Boudicca, also known as Boudica, Boudiccea or Boudicea, lived nearly 2,000 years ago when Britain was part of the Roman Empire.

She was the Queen of the Iceni, an ancient British tribe from East Anglia. When the Romans tried to steal Iceni land and tax the people, Boudicca reportedly raised around 230,000 men to fight against 10,000 Roman soldiers. Somehow the Romans won!

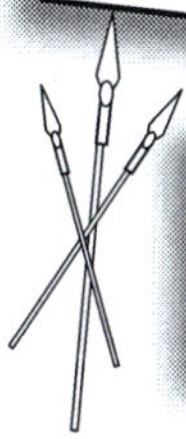

The name 'Boudicca' means 'victory'.

Allegedly, when Boudicca realised her army was going to lose the battle, she killed herself by drinking poison, rather than become a Roman prisoner.

A Roman called Dio Cassius described Boudicca as 'tall', 'terrifying', 'fierce', and 'harsh', but also said she was intelligent. He said she had very long, tawny hair and wore a big gold necklace. She also carried a big spear which made her even more scary!

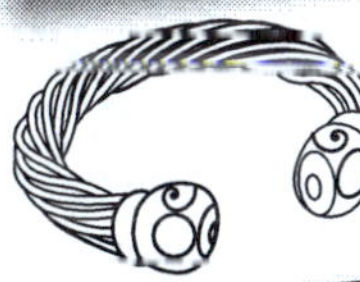

Today, Boudicca, warrior queen of the Iceni, is considered a heroine who stood against the hated Roman invaders. A life-sized statue of her now stands at Westminster Bridge, across from the Houses of Parliament.

Roman Empire

(27 BC – AD 476/1453)

The Romans were responsible for killing many Christians but later they became Christian themselves and the killing stopped.

The Romans came to Britain nearly 2000 years ago (43 AD until 410 AD) and changed our country. Even today, evidence of the Romans being here can be seen in the ruins of Roman buildings, forts, roads and baths found all over Britain.

The Romans were very civilised and their villas had central heating and baths.

Romans loved to make laws, by the end they had written down about 3 million of them. Most of our laws are based on old Roman ones.

In the old Roman calendar there were only 10 months, March was the beginning of the year and there were no months in the winter! The month 'July' is named after the emperor Julius Caesar and 'August' is named after Emperor Augustus.

Pecunia non olet means 'money does not smell'. This phrase was coined as a result of the urine tax charged by the Roman emperors in the 1st century upon the collection of urine. It was used in tanning, and also by launderers as a source of ammonia to clean and whiten woollen togas. There are even isolated reports of it being used as a teeth whitener!

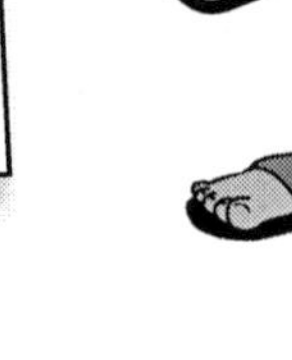

Evacuation Day

I miss it when she says,
'Night, night dear.'

Going to another place to stay,
All the people at the station,
Mum, children and relations,
Breaking into two.

Teddy, snack, clothes and shampoo,
Oh little brother, he doesn't even know what's going on
And when the cloud of smoke disappeared
The light shone.
Tears running from Mother's eyes,
'Quick, run, the bombs are in the skies!'
'Bye,' all the children say,
Into the next day . . . still on their way.

Mr and Mrs Harold
Welcome me, bath me, feed me,
One egg a week
And when I have a sneak peek outside
Argh! a monster!
No -
A cow
Meat from a cow,
How?
Cut, chop!

At night, shut the door,
Oh I feel sore,
Oh. I wish Mum was here.

Evan White (9)
Joy Lane Primary School, Whitstable

Napoleon Bonaparte

(15th August 1769 – 5th May 1821)

After the French Revolution of 1789 had overthrown King Louis XVI, Napoleon rose to power rapidly - he was a military genius with a brilliant command.

He was a short man, with the nickname 'the little corporal'. His rise to power was helped by his first wife, the beautiful Josephine de Beauharnais.

After bringing economic prosperity and peace to France, Napoleon set out to conquer the remainder of Europe. He was able to conquer a significant amount of land.

In 1804 Napoleon crowned himself emperor of the French and received the Pope's blessing.

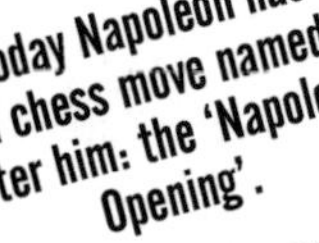

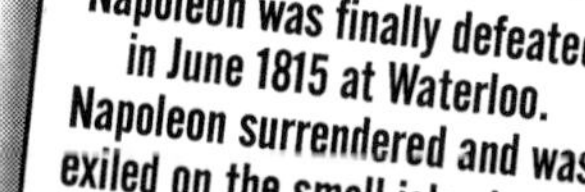

Today Napoleon has a chess move named after him: the 'Napoleon Opening'.

Napoleon was finally defeated in June 1815 at Waterloo. Napoleon surrendered and was exiled on the small island of St Helena.

Joan of Arc

(1412 – 30th May 1431)

Joan of Arc is the youngest person in history to command the armies of a nation. Charles VII officially gave Joan command of the armies of France when she was only 17.

A prophecy foretold that France would be saved by a maid from Lorraine. It was a popular prediction in France during Joan's time and has been attributed to prophets including the mythical Merlin.

Joan of Arc's greatest military victory was at Patay on June 18th, 1429. Joan's army annihilated the English force, killing over 2,000 while suffering almost no losses.

Charles himself drew Joan's coat of arms featuring a sword holding a crown with a fleur-de-lis on each side.

Joan predicted she would be wounded by an arrow in her chest during an attack on the fort Les Tourelles. Her prediction came true and is documented in a letter written by Charles' cousin fifteen days before.

Joan of Arc was officially canonized by Pope Benedict XV on May 16th 1920, under the same church that executed her for heresy.

Vikings

(The late 8th to the mid 11th century)

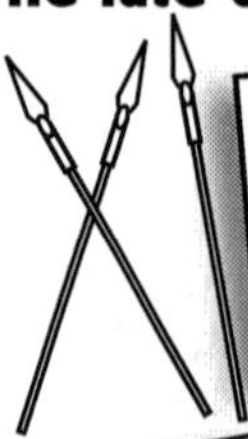

The name 'Viking' means 'a pirate raid' in the Old Norse language.

The Vikings were famous for sailing huge distances. Around 500 years before Christopher Columbus 'discovered' the Americas, Vikings had visited their shores. Leif Ericsson was the one who led the Vikings over to what is now Canada in around AD 1000.

Among the many gods Vikings believed in were Thor, the god of thunder, and Loki, a cheeky mischief-maker who could shape-shift to become all different kinds of animals.

The Vikings were expert boat builders and sailors. They invented 'keels' which made their 'longboats' easy to steer, and because of their design to float high in the water, landing on beaches was easy.

Fenrir Greyback, the werewolf in the Harry Potter books, was named after a ferocious giant wolf from Ancient Viking mythology.

Vegetables in Viking times were much smaller than the ones we enjoy today, they were more like wild plants. Viking carrots were dark purple, not orange!

Victorians

(Queen Victoria's reign lasted from 20th June 1837 until her death on 22nd January 1901)

Britain built a huge empire during the Victorian period. In 1837 most people lived in villages and worked on the land; by 1901, most lived in towns and worked in offices, shops and factories.

Britain became the most powerful and richest country in the world, with the largest empire that had ever existed, ruling a quarter of the world's population.

The number of people living in Britain more than doubled from 16 million to 37 million, causing a huge demand for food, clothes and housing.

There were no painkillers nor anaesthesia for the Victorians – operations went on for hours with patients in excruciating agony.

The police force was created during the Victorian period by Sir Robert Peel (hence the nickname 'Bobbies').

To control insects, many people kept a hedgehog in the basement. It curled up and slept in the day, but roamed around the dark kitchen at night eating cockroaches and other insects.

Children were often forced to work. Many were used as cheap labour in factories, or as chimney sweeps. The work was dangerous and painful. Some boys got stuck and died of suffocation.

Henry VIII & Tudors

(Henry's reign 28th June 1491 – 28th January 1547
Tudor dynasty from 1485 until 1603)

The first Tudor king was Henry VII. He became king after the Battle of Bosworth Field, which ended the Wars of the Roses.

Henry VIII is probably the most well known of the Tudor monarchs. He was a very selfish person and by the end of his life everyone was afraid of him, mainly because of his ruthless behaviour toward anyone who didn't agree with him.

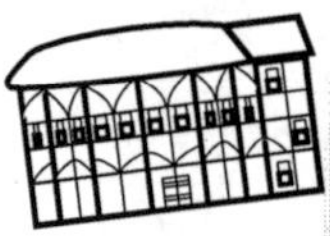

In 1534, Henry VIII broke away from the Catholic Church and proclaimed himself head of the Church of England. Henry sold off the land and riches of the church to dukes, barons and other noblemen.

Contrary to popular opinion, Henry VIII had many children. Unfortunately it was very common in Tudor times for them to die very young. Only three survived beyond childhood.

An average person drank about 8 pints of 'weak beer' a day. It had very little alcohol in it, and even children drank it. It was safer than the water available at the time.

The ending of the marriages of King Henry VIII can be remembered by the following rhyme:
'Divorced, beheaded, died divorced, beheaded, survived'.

Boudicca

Died between 60 and 62 AD

Boudicca, also known as Boudica, Boudiccea or Boudicea, lived nearly 2,000 years ago when Britain was part of the Roman Empire.

She was the Queen of the Iceni, an ancient British tribe from East Anglia. When the Romans tried to steal Iceni land and tax the people, Boudicca reportedly raised around 230,000 men to fight against 10,000 Roman soldiers. Somehow the Romans won!

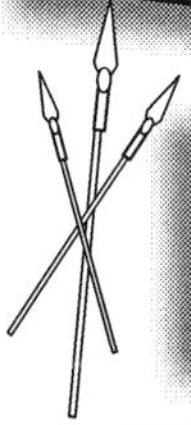

The name 'Boudicca' means 'victory'.

Allegedly, when Boudicca realised her army was going to lose the battle, she killed herself by drinking poison, rather than become a Roman prisoner.

A Roman called Dio Cassius described Boudicca as 'tall', 'terrifying', 'fierce', and 'harsh', but also said she was intelligent. He said she had very long, tawny hair and wore a big gold necklace. She also carried a big spear which made her even more scary!

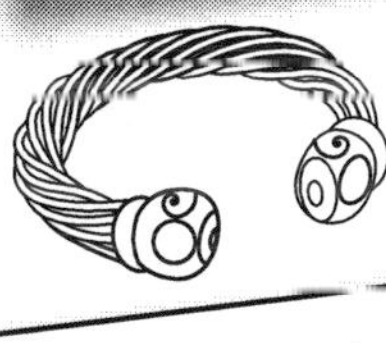

Today, Boudicca, warrior queen of the Iceni, is considered a heroine who stood against the hated Roman invaders. A life-sized statue of her now stands at Westminster Bridge, across from the Houses of Parliament.

Roman Empire

(27 BC – AD 476/1453)

The Romans came to Britain nearly 2000 years ago (43 AD until 410 AD) and changed our country. Even today, evidence of the Romans being here can be seen in the ruins of Roman buildings, forts, roads and baths found all over Britain.

The Romans were responsible for killing many Christians but later they became Christian themselves and the killing stopped.

The Romans were very civilised and their villas had central heating and baths.

Romans loved to make laws, by the end they had written down about 3 million of them. Most of our laws are based on old Roman ones.

In the old Roman calendar there were only 10 months, March was the beginning of the year and there were no months in the winter! The month 'July' is named after the emperor Julius Caesar and 'August' is named after Emperor Augustus.

Pecunia non olet means 'money does not smell'. This phrase was coined as a result of the urine tax charged by the Roman emperors in the 1st century upon the collection of urine. It was used in tanning, and also by launderers as a source of ammonia to clean and whiten woollen togas. There are even isolated reports of it being used as a teeth whitener!

Cleopatra
(69–30 BC)

Cleopatra was a master of 9 languages, and was the only person in the entire Ptolemaic dynasty who could speak Egyptian! Wow!

Cleopatra married 2 of her own brothers, ew!

Historians believe that Cleopatra was not stunningly beautiful, but had an ordinary face with a hooked nose, and 'masculine' features.

Cleopatra wasn't Egyptian; she was Greek.

As Queen, Cleopatra was skilled in the arts of warfare. She was a naval commander, and twice led her fleet in battle.

Cleopatra was extremely charismatic and quick-witted. She was very good at persuading people to do things the way she wanted them.

Cleopatra was 39 years old when she died from the bite of a cobra.

Ancient Egypt

(3150 BC – 30 BC)

Ancient Egyptians had great medical skills. They could set broken bones, perform surgeries, and they even developed anaesthetic.

The Ancient Egyptians developed the toilet seat, combs, scissors, make-up, toothpaste and toothbrushes.

Both men and women in Egypt wore make-up to protect their skin from the hot sun.

The Ancient Egyptians measured one hour as one twelfth of the day between sunrise and sunset. This meant that an hour was much longer in summer than in winter.

Pharaoh Pepi II of Egypt used slaves smeared in honey, to attract flies away from him!

The people of Ancient Egypt divided Egypt into two areas. The 'Red Land' was the deserts that protected both sides of Egypt from neighbouring countries and invading armies. The 'Black Land' was the fertile land near the River Nile where people grew their crops.

Nearly all Ancient Egyptian homes had a cat, but cats were not pets. The Ancient Egyptians believed that cats had magical powers. They believed cats protected their homes and children from danger.

Prehistoric Life

(250 million years ago to about 3200BC)

Prehistoric refers to time preceding both human existence and the invention of writing

At one point, all of the Earth's continents are thought to have been connected as one huge land mass. This one huge 'continent' is known as Pangaea.

Archaeology is the study of past human life and culture by the examination of actual evidence, such as graves, buildings, tools and pottery.

Geology is the study of the origin, history, and structure of the Earth.

The Earth is 4.5 billion years old. It took nearly a billion years for the atmosphere to become stable enough to sustain life.

Palaeontology is the study of fossils of life existing in prehistoric times.

To help fight carnivores, many herbivores had natural weapons at their disposal. Examples of this include the spikes on the tail of the stegosaurus and the three horns attached to the front of the triceratops' head.

The largest tooth of any carnivorous dinosaur found to this date is that of a T-rex. It is estimated to have been around 30cm (12in) long including the root.

The Cretaceous era ended with the mass extinction of the dinosaurs. It's widely believed that an asteroid 6 miles in diameter struck the Earth in the Gulf of Mexico, leaving a crater 150 miles wide.

64 million years after dinosaurs became extinct, humans emerged in the Cenozoic era.

WW2 Evacuation Poem

I was at the train station waiting to be evacuated
People were pushing past me as though I was not there
It was hot and sticky because everyone was crammed together
The smell of sweat was in the air
While mums were crying everywhere
Like one big waterfall
Apart from mine who did not shed a tear
I heard a clattering of the tracks
I saw a puff of cloud
Then it pulled up
The train, to take me and the other children away
To the country
To keep us safe from harm
As all of the other children boarded the train
I was giving my mum a hug
I saw my mum smile
Then I let go
As I boarded the train a whistle came and the train chugged away
I put my head out the window
To see my mum wave goodbye
And I waved back
Finally, my mum shed a tear
And so did I
As the train chugged off into the bright blue sky.

Tristan Quinn (10)
Joy Lane Primary School, Whitstable

WW2 Poem

Mums in misery,
Sweaty children bundled together,
The train is coming in,
Tears dripping down children's faces,
'Children the train is coming!'
'I wonder when the war will be over?'
Children getting on the train,
Some of them don't want to go.

Finley Lambert (9)
Joy Lane Primary School, Whitstable

World War 2

I can hear the noisy steam train,
It sounds like people are in pain,
Everybody, mostly the adults are crying,
Some say they're not, they're lying.

I can see tears rolling down faces,
My mother hasn't taken me places,
I see the train is on its way,
It is here, goodbye for today.

I'm scared, I don't want to die,
I didn't even say a proper goodbye,
There is no one here for me,
It's hard to speak with joy and glee.

I can feel fear in the air,
Nobody seems to care,
My parents are leaving me,
They will be unable to eat their tea.

I got on the train,
In the rain,
I felt like I had a chill,
I sat and waited until . . .

Katy Thomas (10)
Joy Lane Primary School, Whitstable

Evacuation

I can see children waiting solemnly for their train to come by.
Children cry as they wave goodbye to their upset mums.
Children play silly games.
Kids have tags that state their names.

I can feel rushing children pushing me roughly.
I feel like a parcel being delivered to strangers.
I feel scared but excited at the same time
Because I am leaving my mum
But I am going to the countryside
To be safe.

Rachel Cox (9)
Joy Lane Primary School, Whitstable

Evacuation

E vacuation, the worst thing ever,
you could never imagine
V isions come to me
of my sad and upset mother
A t the station tears roll down my face,
I might never see my mother again
C ould I have been born in a different era
because this is such terror?
U nder the train's doorway I wave a sad goodbye
to my mother who cried
A s I passed into the distance
I took one last glimpse at my wonderful mum
T ime has passed very slowly,
for it feels like I've been on the train for 24 hours
I n the town hall I was first to be chosen,
hooray, at last
O n the way to my country town,
I made new friends and had a lot of fun
N ow I'm with a happy family
while the terrible war carries on.

Emily Williams (11)
Joy Lane Primary School, Whitstable

Sad Life

A few weeks ago I said goodbye to my dad,
Now I feel so sad we are being evacuated.
Me and my sis,
This is going to be bliss.
All around people crying, with some people dying.
My mum says this is a holiday,
I know she's lying because she's crying.

The tears on my face trickle down like rain,
My suitcase is only the size of a classroom folder,
It makes me look a little bolder.
The trains are coming in,
The lights start to dim.

Ieuan Jones (10)
Joy Lane Primary School, Whitstable

WW2 Evacuation Poem

The children are waiting,
The mums are crying tears,
Like rain dripping down a window.

I can hear people screaming
And shouting up and down.

I feel my mum's sweaty and sticky hand
Holding onto my arm.

I can smell the steam of the train gush past my nose,
With the smell of sweat,
Just like gas.

I wish I were staying here,
But it's for the best,
Before my brother and me get on the train
My sad mum gives us a wave.

To my surprise we are going to the countryside!

I feel scared inside, I don't want to leave here,
But I'll be back . . .

Jamie-Leigh Freeman (10)
Joy Lane Primary School, Whitstable

The Evacuation

Why am I running?
All I know is the train is coming,
The conductor is shouting,
'All aboard, all aboard!'

Mum is saying, 'Be calm, it's a holiday.'
The palm of her hand is wet with sweat,
She sweats when she's lying,
My mum sighs and knows I'm not buying it.

Mum pushes me aboard the train,
She can't hide all that pain.
I have no idea where I'm going,
All I can do is sit and do nothing.

Daniel Mawardi (10)
Joy Lane Primary School, Whitstable

WW2 To The Countryside

What can you see?
Tears running down the pale skin of the mums' faces,
Tags pinned onto the coats of the children who are being evacuated,
Young children playing like they think it's a holiday,
Gas masks hanging from evacuees' coats,
The steam whooshing by as the train goes fast.

What can you hear?
The train chugging along the railway,
Mums crying as they say goodbye to their sons and daughters,
Children laughing as they think they are going on holiday,
Kids pretending to play aeroplanes and saying, 'Hitler is dead!'

What can you feel?
Heat coming from the steam
And people crowding around me,
Wet palms from mum as she hugs me goodbye.

Lauren Clements (10)
Joy Lane Primary School, Whitstable

Train Station In WW2

I can hear -
I can hear the chugging of the train,
The screaming of happy children playing,
Sad mums crying over babies,
Screeching of brakes on the train.

I can smell -
The smoke of the bombs when they hit the ground,
The smell of petrol because the tank has blown,
The smell of fire from the German bombs.

I can see -
I can see children playing while bombs are falling,
Mums hugging their children
Because they may never see them again
The train coming into the station, being careful by the station.

Joseph Billington (9)
Joy Lane Primary School, Whitstable

The Station

I can see the kids running around their mum,
The steam from the train covers me,
Mum crying like she hasn't before,
I have a tag on my coat, as if I would forget
My name!
I know my dad will be fighting, I don't want him
To get hurt.
I have got a small suitcase,
It can only fit small things in there.
Kids trying to make me feel better.
The train pulls into the station,
I want to get on the train
So I don't have to see my dad get hurt.

Help me!

Louise Petcher (9)
Joy Lane Primary School, Whitstable

It's Hard To Say Goodbye

Tags are seen everywhere,
No matter where you look, they are there.
Some of the children are quite grim,
See mums sobbing, with tears down their face,
For them to watch their kids going is such a disgrace.
The thought of my dad in the war,
I think it's a terrible law.
I see the train going past,
I think it's going really far.
As I get on the train I wave goodbye,
I know my mum really wants to cry.
I arrive at the countryside with my new family,
Hopefully they really like me.

Paige Harris (9)
Joy Lane Primary School, Whitstable

WW2 Evacuation

What can you hear?
Mums crying sadly, saying goodbye to their children.
Little children screaming loudly, running around their mums.
The train whistling as it comes into the station.

What do you feel?
Children budging, while mums are hugging their children.
Kids hitting adults as they play around the station.
The long trains coming into the station to take the children
To their new homes in the countryside.

Upset mums crying on their children's shoulders.
Kids getting on the train and saying goodbye.
Moving away from the bombs dropping on London.

Connor Johncock (10)
Joy Lane Primary School, Whitstable

The Little Boy's Adventure

The station is filled with people,
I can hear the whistle blowing,
But I don't understand!
It's just a holiday and a new place to explore,
It's all so fascinating playing planes as normal,
There is nothing to worry about,
It is all just an adventure,
Just starting,
The train is about to go,
And I know I have to leave to the countryside,
My mum cries as the train leaves,
Knowing she might not see me again.

Katie Dawson (9)
Joy Lane Primary School, Whitstable

Evacuation Poem

I feel as scared as a rabbit being chased by a fox
I've just been told I'm being evacuated.
At the station crowds of people are squashed together
I can smell steam and coal as the train puffs in.
Mothers and children waving goodbye tearfully
As the train leaves the station the whistle blows . . .
When will I see my parents again?
I feel like a parcel on the mail train
My label pinned to my red winter coat.
At the village hall bundles of children waiting to be picked
I hope my host family is kind.

Jade Traveller (9)
Joy Lane Primary School, Whitstable

Evacuee Poem

Children sadly leaving their homes
Aches and pains in their bones
As they carry their brown box
Pulling up their long, white socks
It may be hard to leave Mum and dad
But they'll just think of the good times they had
As they sit and wave goodbye
They try their hardest not to cry
When they arrive at their new place to stay
You can hear the families saying, 'Hip, hip hooray!'

Saphia Lestrade (10)
Joy Lane Primary School, Whitstable

Evacuation

High-pitched children screaming, suitcases
Cardboard labels on long winter coats
Feeling scared like a rabbit being chased by a fox
The station was loud
Trains went through on their way to the countryside.

Isobel Ansett (10)
Joy Lane Primary School, Whitstable

Evacuees

Standing on a station platform
Waiting for our train.

We don't know where we're going
Or where we have to stay.

They say it's for our safety
It won't be for long
We'll miss you very much son
Take care and
Be strong.

Liam Freeman (9)
Joy Lane Primary School, Whitstable

Evacuation

As I wave goodbye to my mum
I hear the siren hoot,
Loudly and clearly, as I see people dashing through the street.
Run, run! People say as I just catch a glimpse
And I see a German aeroplane go under my daddy's feet.
I can hear mums and babies crying
And some having the time of their lives.
I just feel sorry for them
And especially their minds.

Ella Cady (9)
Joy Lane Primary School, Whitstable

Evacuation

You can see the train coming rapidly down the track,
You can see your little brother dancing around,
You can hear mums crying to their kids,
Children saying bye to their mums,
You can feel your suitcase taking the strain,
You can feel your gas mask bouncing on your back.

I feel scared, lost . . .

Oliver Myhill (9)
Joy Lane Primary School, Whitstable

Evacuee Poem

'E very boy and girl being evacuated,' said my mum
V ery scared and feeling down in the dumps as I walk to the station
A s I hear the steam train chugging I know it's time
C hugging, chugging as it comes to a halt, my tears welling up
U sing my strength I hold my tears inside
E very parent is crying as we board the train
E ach child waves as the train puffs out of the station,
not knowing where they are going.

Jack Martin (10)
Joy Lane Primary School, Whitstable

WW2 Evacuees

I can hear the mums crying,
Brothers and sisters shouting out of the windows.
Dad sitting on the benches with injuries,
Mums saying 'It's just a holiday.'
And off the train goes,
With puffs of smoke coming out the chimneys.

Daniel Lee (10)
Joy Lane Primary School, Whitstable

The Magic Box

(Inspired by 'Magic Box' by Kit Wright)

I will put in the box . . .
A ghost going as white as snow,
It is from Greece centuries ago
It is like a shimmering shadow
A magical key glistening in the black.

I will put in the box . . .
A beautiful glistening key.

I will put in the box . . .
A gleaming ancient Greek army

Philip Payne (8)
Nutley CE Primary School, Nutley

The Magic Box

(Inspired by 'Magic Box'; by Kit Wright)

I will put in my box . . .
A shimmering gold sword ready for battle
A fierce flame from the gods
The chance to win every Greek Olympic game.

I will put in my box . . .
The wonder of the Greek sands
The silk of the Greek dresses
Me ruling the Greek universe.

I will put in my box . . .
The secrets that mustn't be told
The armour of a hero
The head of Medusa.

I will put in my box . . .
The chance to defeat the most horrible and evil beast
A soldier in a tunic
A slave with a shield.

My box has . . .
Sharp points sticking out of the top
Leaves sticking out of the box
Spooky eyes on the edge.
Zeus' armour hanging off the bottom
Silk from Athene's dress wrapped around it.
The first speck of daylight is shining on the box.

Olivia Sharif (8)
Nutley CE Primary School, Nutley

The Magic Box

(Inspired by 'Magic Box' by Kit Wright)

I will put in my box . . .
An amazing labyrinth with the worst monsters inside.
The Ancient Zeus as smart as a man going to work.
The very first touch of democracy in Athens.

I will put in my box . . .
A brave scary soldier going to war in a charging chariot.
The Big Bang going *bang!*
Myself as ruler of Greece.

I will put in my box . . .
A clicking ticking tick-tock clock
A gluey glue stick sticking together
A Greek groan of a near dead man.

I will put in my box . . .
A Greek god greeting their daughter or son
Powerful Poseidon praying to his brother
Horrible Hades failing at hypnotising Zeus.

My box has car wheels on the hinges
And the great light of love.
Hate comes to my box.
The whole world is in my big box.
Mountains of jelly hide in the corners of my huge box.

Jonny Rowland (8)
Nutley CE Primary School, Nutley

My Magic Box

(Inspired by 'Magic Box' by Kit Wright)

I will put in my box . . .
Mist rolling in from the lush green hills,
The memories of an old soldier fighting in the war,
A shimmering sun on an old cottage in the forest.

I will put in my box . . .
Soft snowflakes falling from the sky like a magical whirlwind
The fuel of fireworks glittering in the sky
A glimmering silver sword ready for war.

I will put in my box . . .
The shine of the most expensive jewels,
The flame of the first Olympic torch,
A big ship ready to sail.

I will put in my box . . .
A stunning Greek pot in a museum,
A statue of the mighty Zeus
And a great big cup for winning a race.

My box is fashioned with flowers
And there are secrets in the corners
It shines like shields
And when you lick it you taste the best food.
It is the best box for miles.

Sarah Pinner (7)
Nutley CE Primary School, Nutley

The Magic Box

(Inspired by 'Magic Box' by Kit Wright)

I will put in the box . . .
A glimmering silver sword ready for war.
My face on a shiny Greek pot.
A huge, bronze shield.

I will put in the box . . .
A charging warrior with a sword and shield.
A wax tablet ready to use.
Lots of lovely gold pots.

I will put in the box . . .
Athens and Sparta ready for war.
A giant, stunning ship ready to sail.
A black and grey horse galloping through a forest.

I will put in the box . . .
£100,000 and lots of gold.
Me winning the Olympic games and the gold medal.
A Greek warrior wearing a tunic and a woman wearing gold armour.

My box is pictures of the mighty Zeus.
Money stuck to the corners.
The warm glow of the love God Athena.
It is made out of bronze, silver and gold.

Rohan Milne (8)
Nutley CE Primary School, Nutley

The Magic Box

(Inspired by 'Magic Box' by Kit Wright)

I will put in the box . . .
Unlimited love from the beautiful Aphrodite,
The bright flame of the first Olympic torch,
A pure gold sword to fight with.

I will put in the box . . .
A stunning dark as death tunic
All the power I need from the mighty Zeus
A young goat to use for my needs.

I will put in the box . . .
All the meat in need from the mighty Artimes,
Me in Zeus' place,
An incredible labyrinth to play in.

I will put in the box . . .
The ability to defeat my enemies without a war,
The chance to kill everyone with kindness,
A row of Olympic cups.

My box is as black as night
With secrets on the lid,
Gifts from the Gods in the corners
And the Greek crown everlasting.

Eleanor Mumford (8)
Nutley CE Primary School, Nutley

The Magic Box

(Inspired by 'Magic Box' by Kit Wright)

I will put in the box . . .
Me as the owner of all the theatre.
A sip of Aphrodite's fountain of love.
A nice shimmering sword ready to fight.

I will put in the box . . .
Three rows of cups for winning Olympic races.
All the power I need from Zeus.
The most beautiful tunic ever made, with silver sequins.

I will put in the box . . .
A dead goat ready to use its horns.
The beautiful sky with silver stars and a white moon.
If I had powers from Zeus I would click my fingers and all my troubles would disappear.

I will put in the box . . .
A Palomino that gallops through the wind
Thin pure deep blue sea as blue as Dulux paint.

My box is as silver as a star
With gifts from all the gods in the corners
The mighty crown of Zeus.

Ellie Webb (8)
Nutley CE Primary School, Nutley

The Magic Box

(Inspired by 'Magic Box' by Kit Wright)

I will put in the box . . .
Athene in shining armour,
A beautiful crown and a soldier's smile.

I will put into the box . . .
The first Olympic's trophy,
A mythical creature running away.

My box
Looks like gold, silver, silver and gems.

Amy Hoadley (8)
Nutley CE Primary School, Nutley

The Magic Box

(Inspired by 'Magic Box' by Kit Wright)

I will put in the box . . .
A boiling sun
A big shield
A glimmering sword.

I will put in the box . . .
Hades' fire
A wax tablet
Greek vases.

I will put in the box . . .
Greek pottery
A busy Greek school.

I will put in the box . . .
An outdoor theatre
A Greek boat
Golden drachma.

My box is covered in stripes
And pretty flowers growing on an island.

Luke Creenan (8)
Nutley CE Primary School, Nutley

The Magic Box

(Inspired by 'Magic Box' by Kit Wright)

I will put in the box . . .
The cry of the first baby
A beautiful setting sun
The roar of an army ready for war.

I will put in the box . . .
A white horse galloping through the woods,
An army man in a mother's arms
A baby in war.

I will put in the box . . .
10,000 drachmas
The first fruit from a tree
A great emperor
The wing from an ancient animal
The god Hephaeslus warm with fire
The first marriage of Zeus.

My box is covered with gold stars with a bronze lock
And a granite lid.

Luca Falletti (9)
Nutley CE Primary School, Nutley

The Magic Box

(Inspired on 'Magic Box' by Kit Wright)

I will put in my box . . .
A big galloping horse galloping on the beach.
A Greek man with shining armour.
A silver sword ready for war,
A man climbing up a stormy mountain.

I will put in my box . . .
A big boat that can sail around 15 miles.
A new life of a Greek Aphrodite,
A golden Greek island.

I will put in my box . . .
A pot that is round and orange
For the gods to drink out of,
A sun with a picture of the ancient wars,
A big heavy reading book about the battle of Sparta,
A bright red tunic for people to wear.

My box is Greek and it has Greek people and Greek animals,
And lots of other exciting things!

Rosina Petracopoulos (8)
Nutley CE Primary School, Nutley

The Magic Box

(Inspired by 'Magic Box' by Kit Wright)

I will put in the box . . .
A great warrior in a beautiful, shiny tunic
A very pretty and very expensive tunic.

I will put in the box . . .
Zeus wearing a golden tunic
And Athene wearing silver armour.

I will put in the box . . .
A sandy beach with calm seas.

I will put in the box . . .
A lion with golden armour
And a human with a lion's fur.

My box is like shining armour
And a silky dress in a king's palace

Jon Jon Smith (8)
Nutley CE Primary School, Nutley

Attack Of The Dinosaurs

The dinosaurs are roaring
The pterodactyls are soaring
The T-rectos are fighting
They smashing and biting.
They are ripping and chewing the flesh from their prey.

The rocks are crumbling,
They're falling and tumbling.
Each creature hears
As gigantosaurus appears.
The triceratops is charging
It's pushing and barging.
It tries to escape from the cold-blooded killer.

When the predator gets its prey
It munches away.
But the scavengers come when it goes away.

Luke Batty (9)
Oakfields Montessori School, Upminster

The Fall Of Icarus

Daedalus, the craftsman and inventor of old,
He was the best and most famous,
Everyone came to him in Athens
Until he took on Talos.

Talos invented many things,
The first saw and the potter's wheel.
Daedalus was so jealous
He decided he had to kill.

Daedalus was banished from Athens
Along with his son.
They took refuge in Crete,
But were thrown in the Maze Prison.

Finally Daedalus came up with a plan,
A fine and miraculous thing.
His idea was to gather feathers
And fly with birds' wings.

They escaped from the maze,
For miles they flew,
But soon, sadly,
Icarus' death was due.

Icarus' wings melted and broke
As he flew too near the sun.
Poor Daedalus, the craftsman
Had to say goodbye to his son.

Eleanor Gouldie (9)
Oakfields Montessori School, Upminster

Child's Life

Victorians
Silent, gloomy,
Walking, schooling, working
Sick of stitching sacks
Workhouse.

Lucy Calvert (8)
Oakfields Montessori School, Upminster

Ancient Egypt

In ancient Egypt
The pyramids stood,
Tall and proud
For as long as they could.
Inside the pyramid
There lay a tomb
And inside the tomb
Was Ceops, our mighty king.

The sand is white,
The sky is blue,
The sun would shine
Over Pharaoh's tomb, our mighty king.

Our Pharaoh, Ceops
Wore lots of gold,
All the gold
That he could hold, our mighty king.

So everyone worshipped
Ceops, our mighty king,
For wearing lots and
Lots of bling!
So that is all I
Have to say,
Remember what we
Have learnt today.

Imogen Williams (10)
Oakfields Montessori School, Upminster

Noisy Romans - Haiku

Crashing and bashing
The stampeding Romans come
It is frightening.

Crashing and bashing
Murdering and pillaging
Surging around me.

Samuel Priestley (8)
Oakfields Montessori School, Upminster

The Greeks

Mount Olympus their home
The highest mountain in Greece
The radiant Temple of Zeus
Golden palaces

The king of the gods, Zeus
With his symbol, a lightning bolt
God of sky, sea and wind
Strong and mighty

The goddess of Athens
Warfare, wisdom and art
Her favourite plant, an olive tree
Her favourite bird, an owl

Aphrodite, her symbol a dove
The goddess of love
Born on the sea's foam
Was carried by zephyrs to Cyprus

God of the seas, Poseidon
Water as well
Armed with his hunting trident
Bringer of earthquakes.

Gabrielle Bean (9)
Oakfields Montessori School, Upminster

King Zeus

King Zeus!
Sitting proud upon Mount Olympus.
Ruler of the Ancient Greek world -
Strong, mighty, majestic!
As fierce as a caged tiger,
As bright and dazzling as lightning.
He makes me cower away from his omnipotent power.
Like Theseus confronting the fearsome Minotaur.
King Zeus!
Reminding me of an ancient civilisation.

Max Kavanagh (10)
Oakfields Montessori School, Upminster

The Titanic

Through the midnight sea sailed the Titanic
The band kept playing their music
This event was terribly tragic
The boat was gigantic

They said the boat was unsinkable
Titanic was extremely vulnerable
To get to New York Titanic was unable
What happened that night became truly memorable

The party went on
Just a little way to go
Too few lifeboats brought along
When Titanic sank

They had left Southampton Town
Never expecting to strike the ice
Until the boat went down
And so many lost their lives

When the boat sank
It was terrible
They all had many packages and trunks
This story will be history forever more.

Mia Hart (10)
Oakfields Montessori School, Upminster

Coming Of Rome

The Romans are roaring,
The swords are clashing,
The shields protect them from the smashing.

The thought of dying was scary,
But winning was the only aim,
This was the way to power and fame.

Look out for their ships you Britons,
When the thunder on the sea is crashing
And the lightning flashing.

James Sevant (9)
Oakfields Montessori School, Upminster

The Twelve Olympians

The twelve Olympians were the best
Never once were they a pest.
Zeus' dad was very mad
For he ate his children
And that was bad.

Zeus' mum was very smart
For switching Zeus for a rock
Cronos ate it
How yummy it tasted
Or disgusting.

Cronos was shocked
When he saw Zeus.
He didn't know what to say
Except, 'Who are you?'
Awkward moment.

When the twelve Olympians
Fought the Titans
Cronos lost and Zeus won
And the world was settled.

Kareena Kalar (10)
Oakfields Montessori School, Upminster

Medusa

Medusa is ugly, but don't stare
Because of her strands of snaky hair.
She turned people into stone,
But that left her all alone.
That was till Perseus came along,
He was standing tall and strong
And although he was not clad
In all the armour that he had,
He could see her face revealed
And chopped her head off
Looking in his shield.

Arvin Panesar (8)
Oakfields Montessori School, Upminster

The Olympic Games

Side by side the athletes stood
Ready to take on the world.
The races won, the battle fought
For laurels round heads curled.

Boxing
Each pair has to beat the other
Till they are cut and fall.
One winner claims the victory,
The toughest of them all.

Racing in armour
They run with heavy helm and spear,
To win and hear the people cheer.

Horse racing
More dangerous when riders fall,
But worth the risk for the crowd's call.

Discus
Flying like a tiny world
When the spinning discus is hurled.

Harry Millsom (9)
Oakfields Montessori School, Upminster

Disaster - Haikus

Air raid siren sounds
Run to my air raid shelter
Crying for all clear

Bombs drop on buildings
When we look out from shelter
Our house has been bombed

Set off on steam train
I don't want to leave my home
Sent to family.

Emily Kinder (8)
Oakfields Montessori School, Upminster

Our Friend The Odyssey

Oh dear, brave Odysseus
Sailing boldly through the sea.
Terrors and fates held them sailing so long,
Good Odysseus staying strong.

Oh dear, brave Odysseus,
Sailing slowly to his fate.
Further and further with his crew,
Eating Circe's fruit and the Cyclops' stew.

Oh dear, brave Odysseus,
Sailing to defeat evil.
Happy in the sun and free,
One day he will have to pay the fee.

Oh dear, brave Odysseus,
Alas will fail but rise again.
Abominably by the sea defeated,
Then on Ithaca's throne once more seated.

Morgaine Puttergill (9)
Oakfields Montessori School, Upminster

The Birth Of Hercules

Helpless and still he lay,
With comfort and warmth he would stay.
His father, Zeus, up in the clouds,
Watching his child down below.
His human mother, Alcmene, couldn't know
He would be the strongest man.

Hercules, great Zeus' son,
Fought the many-headed Hydra and won,
He killed the Nemean Lion
And wore its coat.
He travelled to the underworld
In Chaeron's boat.
But first of all, while in his cot
He squeezed and squeezed some snakes a lot.

Hanah Ansari (9)
Oakfields Montessori School, Upminster

The Mummification Of Tutankhamun

The mummification of Tutankhamun,
The mummification of our king,
I remember the pushing and shoving
To see Pharaoh's body.

The first day they took out the organs,
The liver, intestines and brain.
But they kept the heart for the weighing
And I watched them salt the body.

They rubbed our king with palm wine,
They covered him in Natron,
They we all waited forty days
To see him wrapped in his coffin and sarcophagus.

I did not see where they hid our lord,
In a tomb in the Valley of the Kings.

Hamzah Kader (9)
Oakfields Montessori School, Upminster

King Henry VIII

There was a king who had six wives,
Three of whom lost their lives.
When Henry got tired
These women's lives expired.
Except Catherine Parr who survived.

Three Catherines, two Annes and a Jane
To give him his one main aim,
He ditched them all one by one,
Until; he finally got his son.

So in the end you see,
He was never really happy.
He ate and ate and ate,
So that became the end of Henry the Eighth.

Jack Callow (10)
Oakfields Montessori School, Upminster

Raiders

The longship sailed slowly to the shore,
Newly designed and crafted.
Huge, colossal and gigantic!
Sailing like a fish,
Reaching like a mighty skyscraper -
Sending shivers down my spine.
I feel frightened . . . miniscule . . . insignificant.
The longship sailed to the shore
Reminding us of the dramatic Viking era.

Patrick Mulroy-Yourell (10)
Oakfields Montessori School, Upminster

Hera

Hera!
Queen of gods.
Powerful, ruling, elegant.
As beautiful as a diamond,
A shining pearl glistening in the heaves.
She makes me feel proud to be female.
Like a queen, sitting on her grand throne.
Hera!
Reminding me of the power of beauty.

Aliya Dalvi (10)
Oakfields Montessori School, Upminster

The Great Battle Of Badr

The great battle
Happened in the 500s.
Bloodthirsty, destructive, vicious,
Like a forgotten sight,
Like the sun shining triumphantly.
I feel anxious when I hear it - like a mother losing her child.
The *great* battle!
Reminds us that violence is never the answer.

Zain Ahmed Ansari (10)
Oakfields Montessori School, Upminster

Hitler

Hitler,
Wiped out millions,
Evil, charismatic, sly.
As evil as the Devil himself.
As cunning as a fox.
I feel angry and I feel bewilderment,
As confused as a fish caught in a net.
Hitler . . .
The Devil.

Henry O'Leary (10)
Oakfields Montessori School, Upminster

The Air Raid Siren

Smell smoke around me
Close my eyes and fear alive
I hear the air raid sirens.

Amelia O'Leary (8)
Oakfields Montessori School, Upminster

Romans - Haiku

Sharp things around me
Heavy armour I now wear
Slaughtering people.

William Marchall (8)
Oakfields Montessori School, Upminster

Knights

Gallant, chivalrous
Battling, jousting, protecting
Knights of the Round Table.

Alexander-James Stump
Oakfields Montessori School, Upminster

Egypt - Haiku

Pyramid in sand
Underneath the mummy lies
Mummification.

Charlotte Todd (8)
Oakfields Montessori School, Upminster

The Coliseum - Haiku

Bodies on the ground
Gladiators fighting death
Blood, guts and glory.

Rueben Kalar (8)
Oakfields Montessori School, Upminster

Romans And Celts - Haiku

The Celts are coming
The fierce Romans are waiting
The big battle starts.

Dylan Almeida (8)
Oakfields Montessori School, Upminster

Egypt - Haiku

Blazing sun around
Pyramids huge and golden
Everywhere sand flies.

Morgan Snyman (8)
Oakfields Montessori School, Upminster

Evacuation - Haiku

Packed lunch, hug goodbye
Shuffle feet, Lime Street Station
Terror on the train.

Ella Shore (8)
Oakfields Montessori School, Upminster

Dinosaur Dinner

Bang, crash! A foot appeared,
A caveman stood and scratched his beard.
'I wonder how to catch that beast,
Which surely would make a lovely feast.'
From his pocket he pulled his knife,
Licked his lips and called his wife.
'I'll start with fire,' she screeched out loud,
'If you catch a dinosaur you will make me proud.'
The dinosaur looked all around
And saw the caveman on the ground.
The caveman called his brothers, near and far,
His grandad and his papa.
The cavemen stood there, spears in hand,
'Let's get our lunch and get it canned.'
From their brows was dripping water,
In anticipation of the slaughter.
Their spears went up into the air
And missed the dinosaur by a hair.
It ran off in such a fright
And disappeared into the night.
'You fools, you idiots, look what you have done,
You scared the thing off and now it has run.
The dinosaur's gone and it's all your fault,
All that's left is beans and salt.'

Carenza Smith (10)
Plumpton Primary School, Plumpton Green

The Victorians

Sitting down with a frown on her face,
Fay picked and poked at her new pencil case.
'*Anything* but history!' Fay would say,
'Anything!' until this one special day.
The pen on the paper filled and mind,
She felt all gentle, all peaceful and kind.
She sank into her poem or so it seemed,
It felt like a long and interesting dream.

A shimmer of light and a gurgle of rhyme,
Fay was filled with the journey of time.

'The Victorians!' Fay breathed with wonder in her voice,
Was it by chance or was it by choice?
The girls sitting sewing, the boys big and strong,
The responsible adults working all day long.
A tear came to her eye as she saw their feet.
All bony and bare like some old dry meat.
Over the fire in a bubbling pot,
Stewed lamb bones all sweaty and hot.
There outside the little ones played,
Banned from the house for most of the day.
Their mother wore a tattered old shawl
And barely noticed her children at all;
Her back bent and battered, she shuffled around,
Her dark black eyes never leaving the ground.

A shimmer of light and a gurgle of rhyme,
Fay was back to her normal time.

There was her teacher striding to and fro,
These dreams and adventures he'll never know.
Unless by chance he reads Fay's rhyme
And realises with surprise that she's travelled in time.

Jasmine Pearce (11)
Plumpton Primary School, Plumpton Green

The Tale Of Queen Victoria

Poor Prince William died one day
Because he was really sick
All his children died before
So along came young Queen Vic!

When she was queen things did change
With the invention of machines with steam,
So who would do the dirty work?
Of course! Poor children, oh how mean!

The rich kids went to school all day,
The poor ones had to toil,
Up the chimneys and down the mines,
Covered in soot and soil.

The telephone, the flushing loo,
Were some of their inventions.
But when they thought of dynamite
It ended all their good intentions.

X-rays, the underground and some cars,
Radio, film and fuse,
After sixty-four years of ruling an empire
You would think she'd be amused!

Lily Halward (10)
Plumpton Primary School, Plumpton Green

The Victorian Children

Children in Victorian times
Had it really tough,
The teachers were very rough,
They had the power to beat
Anyone who was a cheat.

The poor ones worked in factories,
Or were forced up chimneys.
Where they got sooty knees,
Even children as young as five
Had to work to keep alive.

Isobel Oxenbury (10)
Plumpton Primary School, Plumpton Green

World War 2

1939, a sad time for many
In this year World War 2 began

Adolph Hitler, a dictator in Germany
Killed I don't know how many

Ann Frank, just one of those Jews whom he cruelly killed
Just because he wanted a 'pure' race country

So many children were evacuated to the countryside
Who had to leave their mums behind
Didn't return for many years until the war was over

As the sirens were heard many ran for shelter
From the German bombers destroying their homes

60 million people lost their lives in World War 2
Which ended in 1945

A time of celebration, a time to remember
All those who fought and lost their lives.

Helena Smith (9)
Plumpton Primary School, Plumpton Green

Horrible Histories

Stone Age people loved raw meat
All of them had dirty feet.

The Emperors were really cruel,
They didn't like their people at all.

Mummification was very gory,
We all like a horror story.

Henry VIII had lots of wives,
Some beheaded, some survived.

Georgian wigs were hot and big,
They hated noisy little kids.

World War I was big and scary,
Some of them believed in fairies.

Katie-May Bridges (8)
Plumpton Primary School, Plumpton Green

Henry VIII's Wives

First was Catherine of Aragon, very wise she was,
She had a little girl who was the boss.

Second was Anne Boleyn,
She was beheaded, oh what a sin.

Then was Jane Seymour,
She died and was no more.

Next was Anne of Cleves, who Henry divorced,
Then she lived in Lewes because she was forced.

Catherine Howard came next, wife number five,
She lost her head, so she was not alive.

And last, but not least, was Catherine Parr,
She survived, so was the luckiest by far.

Bethany Bowen (10)
Plumpton Primary School, Plumpton Green

Victorians

The rich Victorians lived in lovely homes,
Some had amazing domes.
Some of the poor had to live on the street,
They had no money and nothing to eat.

Victorian children wrote with chalk on slates,
They ate their food from metal plates,
The toys they played with were hoops and sticks,
They got up to lots of tricks!

Young boys were made to work in mines,
It was scary, dark and dangerous sometimes.
Girls worked in big factories every day,
It was hard and dirty and they had little pay.

Lucy Hibberd (10)
Plumpton Primary School, Plumpton Green

Dinosaurs

A long time ago
Dinosaurs go
Around the world in all those years
Some were big, some were small, some were the size of deer!

The T-rex was fierce and strong and ate meat,
He was very tall and had big feet.
The pterodactyl had wings up to 40 feet long,
They soared through the skies with their wings so strong!
Discovered so far over 700 breeds,
Like velociraptors that had a lot of speed!

I love dinosaurs, the big and the small,
The short, fat, skinny, scary and tall!

Abigail Cook (10)
Plumpton Primary School, Plumpton Green

Tomorrow

Sitting on my bed,
Thinking what I dread,
'Is Daddy on his way
And is he OK
Or lying on the ground
Fire all around?'

With my candle burning brightly,
Whizzes and bangs do frighten me.
Planes flying and crashing,
All dogs yapping.
Tomorrow on the train
Life will never be the same.

Ottylia Norman (10)
Plumpton Primary School, Plumpton Green

Travel Back In Rhyme To Hever Castle

Hever Castle is in Kent,
Which is where Anne Boleyn came and went.
Anne Boleyn was a queen
And Henry the Eighth was a dirty rascal.
King Henry the Eighth had six wives
And for most of them it ended ugly
But for the few lucky ones it was fair play!
The castle was built in thirteen hundred;
There is a maze and a lake
So always have a camera to take.
Hever castle is so sweet
And I think it's really neat!

Bobby Lewis (10)
Plumpton Primary School, Plumpton Green

An Unknown World

The squawk of the pterodactyl,
The snarl of the velociraptor,
From the diplodocus to the slithering snake
What a brilliant make.

No one knows for sure
The wonders galore
Of the magnificent tyrannosaur.

A weird and wonderful race,
From one little trace,
Of a bone
In a little stone.

Liberty Metcalfe (10)
Plumpton Primary School, Plumpton Green

World War II

I saw the guns, I saw the light
The men on the battlefield ready to fight
A boom, a bang as the bomb hit the ground
My heart and my head started to pound
I knew that my last words would be
'Tell my kids and my wife to remember me!'
I thought of the wives left at home
Crying as they sadly started to comb
Their child's hair ready to put them to bed
Another night with their father dead.

Aphra Richardson (9)
Plumpton Primary School, Plumpton Green

Roman Rampage

The Romans were frightening,
They rampaged through the Celts' bases.
They drew red blood that made a red river.
Their army was too powerful,
They were too rich
Because they stole gold and riches
To expand their empire
But Barbarian hordes took over and all was lost!

Jacob Gilbert (9)
Plumpton Primary School, Plumpton Green

Florence Nightingale

Florence Nightingale, oh Florence Nightingale
Lady with the lamp
Or rats might call her a tramp
She sorted out British hospitals
In the First World War
Clearing up the blood and guts and gore
Instead of chopping of arms, legs and limbs
She treated us all with a syringe.

Lily Tregenza (10)
Plumpton Primary School, Plumpton Green

The Viking Warrior

I am a Viking warrior,
My name is Mighty Egor.

I am from Norway and I smell
Like a boar.

A scary, hairy forty year old,
Sailing on longboats over the sea
To kill lots of people in England.

Bridie Clift (8)
Plumpton Primary School, Plumpton Green

Victorians

Horses going round the town
Clip clop
The smell of horse poo blowing around
Gas joining in the sound
Boats bobbing up and down
Trains whizzing in the race
Horses walk to every place.

Lottie Bailey (9)
Plumpton Primary School, Plumpton Green

Henry VIII

Henry VIII took so many lives,
In fact he beheaded two of his wives,
He chopped off their heads,
Left them for dead,
Then put them in their underground beds.

Toby Wride (11)
Plumpton Primary School, Plumpton Green

Mean-Blooded Killer

She was a lion ready to pounce,
A cold-blooded killer.
With hair like strands of glowing fire.
A Celtic angel but a Roman Devil.
Her javelin was a swordfish,
A newly sharpened knife,
Point shining,
Wood nailed,
Paint clean and bright.
It hit like a meteor,
Bursting through the skin,
Blood and guts flying
And everyone was dying
And Boudicca was the cause of it all.

Elise Ferris (10)
Queen Boudica Primary School, Colchester

That Is Her, Queen Boudicca

Eyes like roaring flames,
A ninja waiting for a signal of death.
Her shield like a tortoise shell defending,
A troll crushing all who do not bow.
Like death griping for revenge.
A chariot is a herd of bulls,
Her heart is a trumpet.
A dagger is a thunderstorm,
A cape is a sea of blood.
Her howl is like a wolf
And that is her.

Samuel Floodgate (10)
Queen Boudica Primary School, Colchester

Cold-Blooded Killer

Cold-blooded killer,
Her hair like fire,
Eyes as fierce as a tiger,
Her heart is steel.
She is a lion in disguise,
Her dagger is as sharp as a shark's tooth.
A blood-sucking vampire,
Pouncing into the Romans' bodies,
Spear shimmering in the moonlight.

Who is she?

Molly de Smith (10)
Queen Boudica Primary School, Colchester

A Killer Nightmare

Her tourque is as golden as the sun
Spear a flying nightmare
Like rhinos charging towards you
Eyes like red fire
Hair a sea of blood
Her dagger sprinted and stuck into the Romans' hearts
The Celtic Queen but Roman death fear
The death of dead
Cold-blooded killer
Killing nightmare.

Sophie Clinch (10)
Queen Boudica Primary School, Colchester

Cold Killer

Her heart was cold as ice
Flowing red hair dancing with anger
Cloak flowing in the wind
Voice fiery
She was as fierce as fireworks just ready to explode
Who is it?

Jorja Raynham (10)
Queen Boudica Primary School, Colchester

The Roman Devil And The Celt Angel

She bleeds with anger,
She is as fast as lightning,
Her sword drips with Roman blood,
She is as fierce as a crocodile waiting for her prey.
She is thirsty for Roman souls,
She is a viper suffocating her prey.
She is a devil in Roman eyes.
Her name is . . .
Queen Boudica!

Amber Fisher (10)
Queen Boudica Primary School, Colchester

Queen Boudicca

Heart is like an iceberg
Hair is like a red pool of blood
Eyes like black holes
Her dagger was a cold-blooded killer
Shiny red hair danced in the wind
Angry as a lion eating its prey
Swords ran into soldiers' hearts
She's a strike of lightning on a cold, frosty night
She is a thunderstorm on the darkest night.

Lia Waite (9)
Queen Boudica Primary School, Colchester

The Roman Devil

Hair as red as Romans' blood
Her tourque shone brightly in the sun
Stone cold heart
The wind from the sky
Her spear shimmered in the moonlight
Her javelin was a flying nightmare
She was a hard rock
Boudicca had her fun.

Stephanie Jones (9)
Queen Boudica Primary School, Colchester

Boudicca's Rampage

Her tourque as golden as a crown,
Cloak like a rainbow,
Dagger as sharp as a shark's tooth.

She's a Roman Devil
But a Celtic angel.

Her chariot sprinting rapidly,
Her hair is a sea of blood,
She is a lion.

Logan Pigram (9)
Queen Boudica Primary School, Colchester

The Celtic Devil

As tall as a tree
She had long, red, fiery hair
The fury of a rhino
Her spear slept in soldiers' hearts
A killer sword
She was the Devil's fear
The heart of the Devil
The death of the day.

Molly Fraser (9)
Queen Boudica Primary School, Colchester

The Revenge

Her shield a brick wall
Her spear a flying nightmare
Her heart as cold as ice
She was a human terminator
Her hair was like a phoenix
Her eyes were a bowl of flames
She was a snake
A cold-blooded killer.

Jordan Millward (10)
Queen Boudica Primary School, Colchester

Roman Nightmare

She was the Romans' worst nightmare
Her eyes black as death
Hair red as Hell
A furious dagger ready to pounce wildly
A vicious lion ready to strike
Heart of steel
She was the Romans' worst nightmare.

Dylan De'ath (9)
Queen Boudica Primary School, Colchester

Royal

She is a Celtic devil searching for more opponents,
Colder than a snowball,
As nasty as thunder and lightning.
She is a pact being broken,
A fast and furious chariot,
She is a spear flying in the air.
Watch out!

Craig Smith (11)
Queen Boudica Primary School, Colchester

The Royal Devil

Her eyes are like roaring flames in the wind,
She is a vampire preparing for the moonlight to come down.
She is the thunder in the sky,
Her heart jumps when she sees death.
She is a snake strangling all in its path,
She is an ogre, ready to stamp on those who do not bow down to her
And that is Boudicca!

Toni-Lea Poll (9)
Queen Boudica Primary School, Colchester

The Plague Of The Romans

Her hair is like a sea of blood,
Anger spread like wildfire,
Worse than the plague.
She's as cold as a snowball,
The Devil from the underworld,
Her dagger is as sharp as a lion's tooth,
A wolf hunting for its prey.

George Lennox (11)
Queen Boudica Primary School, Colchester

The Celtic Angel

Eyes as blue as the sky
Necklace as gold as the hot sun
Blood-red hair
Her chariot is like a tank
Celtic angel
Roman Devil!

Oliwer Pilecki (10)
Queen Boudica Primary School, Colchester

Soldier In World War II

Wounded soldiers on the ground
Flying Spitfires all around

Sad soldiers crying loud
Huge tanks make loud sounds

Soldiers feel the deep, dark mud
Soldiers falling with a thud

Soldiers feeling the wet rain
Along with a giant plane

Crashing bombs here and there
Soldiers shouting to take care.

Madison Golding (8)
St Botolph's CE (VA) Primary School, Northfleet

World War Two Blues

Injured soldiers crying, weeping,
Chimney sweepers, running, sweeping.
Bombs falling form the sky,
German planes whizzing by.

I feel scared, I feel afraid,
In the dark shelter
Because of an air raid.

My home's been bombed,
My friends have died,
There are too many bombs outside.

I feel hurt, angry, sad,
I am worried, feeling bad.
I see a soldier with a gun,
Everyone, let's run, run, run!

Maria Nyasha Mukaronda (9)
St Botolph's CE (VA) Primary School, Northfleet

Soldiers In World War II

Huge tanks aiming high,
Shining bombs in the sky.

Rubble all over the hard ground,
The dirty Spitfires all around.

Soldiers feeling very sad,
Covered in mud, that's too bad.

Rain on your back,
Aching shoulders from your pack.

The rattle of the machine gun,
People shouting as they run.

Amy Price (8)
St Botolph's CE (VA) Primary School, Northfleet

Children In The War

I can see children roaring with guns
And little children eating jam buns.

I can see massive army tanks,
People hiding behind big banks.

I can hear noises like a rocket
And banging my head on a magnet.

I can see a wounded soldier
And big boulders all around.

Tomas Hrabe (8)
St Botolph's CE (VA) Primary School, Northfleet

The Victorian Street

I see thick, dark smoke puffing above my head,
The constant spin, turn, twirl of the grubby, oily machinery.
Sooty little boys crawl in and out of the gloomy grey chimneys,
They look uncomfortable, troubled and miserable
Like it's all too much for them.

I hear screams of pain as small children make grabs for bits of cotton
And their limbs are brutally sliced off.
People coughing and wheezing after breathing in the horror
That fills the manky, old air.

I sense the diseases around me, the need to cough.
I sense the cruelty these children are put through
And worst of all I feel the starvation,
The poor people about me.
The starvation that has power over them,
Making them do almost anything for food.

I can smell the horse droppings from the street,
The smoke from people's tobacco,
The evil whiff of the fishmonger's wares
And smelly perfumes of the rich.

This is a Victorian street,
How things have changed.

Marty Edmeades (10)
St Philomena's Primary School, Orpington

My Name Is Harry

My name is Harry
My sister is Emma
My mum died in childbirth
My dad is very poor, he works in a coal mine
Most of the time I'm on my own
My sister is really ill because of the bad diseases
We only have a quarter of bread each and watered down beer,
Sometimes milk
My teacher is not very nice, she stinks like onions
She makes me do hard work and she whips me a lot
My friend Tom is poor too
We play in the street, racing iron hoops
Tom's dad is a farmer
He sometimes gives us a little bit of meat
It is delicious
I have to do a few jobs
I have to collect water in a leather bucket
It is really hard to hold because all the water comes out the holes
I only have a bath once a year
And I have to share the water with my family
There are lots of horses and carts
I am scared of the dark but I have to blow my candle out
As it has to last a month
There are very smoky places near the factories
There are not many shops but there are a lot of pubs
Lots of babies die because their mums have no food for them
More and more people die because the smoky places are really bad
Bye now, I have to go and collect some coal from the street . . .

Zoe Cutts (9)
St Philomena's Primary School, Orpington

I Don't Understand

Dad left, Mum always crying,
I'm worried, I don't understand.
We rush to the cold, full air raid shelter,
I'm confused, I don't understand.
I hear sirens, full blasting engines,
I'm scared, I don't understand.
I peek outside, dust, flashing lights,
What's going on? I don't understand.
My blood shivers, chills down my spine,
Firemen rushing, I don't understand.
It's exhilarating, is it supposed to be fun?
I'm not happy, I don't understand.
It's stopped, it is over?
We're not going out, I don't understand.
It starts again, more utter horror,
Everyone's huddled up, I don't understand.
I'm squashed in the small bunkbed,
No one's actually asleep, I don't understand.
Heart thumping, oh wait, it stops again,
We go in the damp, dark, forgotten house, I don't understand.
Mum tells me I have to leave,
We pack my things, I don't understand.
We go to the station the next day,
I leave, why? I really do not understand

Kayleigh Nimmo (10)
St Philomena's Primary School, Orpington

Victorians

I can see many people on the busy street,
With people riding their horses and carriages.

I can smell the smoke being carried away by the wind
From the towering factory towers.

I can feel the cold air and a whip slapping me
As the owner of the factory urges me to work faster.

Kai Costa (9)
St Philomena's Primary School, Orpington

Never Trust A Victorian Candle

I woke up in my itchy hay bed, the sun is gently rising,
It's warmly shining on my face.
I turn to look at my old, splintery desk
And I can see my candle is still on.
I must blow it out or I'll get a nasty wigging from mother, or worse,
But my eyesight is blurry at this time of morning,
I can't see it properly and if I try to blow it out I might burn myself.
Perhaps I will go and wash my face at the old well,
And maybe I will be able to see it better.
So I climb down the ladder, as my room is in the attic,
Then I go down the stairs.
I put on my slippers and coat.
I do not want to walk the muddy way
Or my mum will see I've been outside.
So I will go through Mr Mesh's garden.
Finally I am at the well,
I run the cold water down my face.
As I am coming back I hear the birds sing their songs.
I wish my father was here but he is in a war,
But I don't think he is coming back.
On my way I bump into my mum and she has got the belt in her hand
And tells me off by whipping me with the horrid belt.
And I can still see the candle in the house.
How I hate that candle.

Grace Pronger (10)
St Philomena's Primary School, Orpington

Victorian People

I see the sad, exhausted servants struggling to work any longer.
I see the poor children having to go up the dark, dusty chimneys.

I hear the children singing as they go to school.
I hear the water splash as the mothers get water from the river.

I feel the soft, flat dough as I make bread.
I feel the pitter-patter of the rain on my face.

Jade Addae-Bosompra (9)
St Philomena's Primary School, Orpington

Roman Times

I am travelling back in Roman times
I can see
People fighting in the amphitheatre
The red tiles on the roof
And the people cheering Rome

I am travelling back in Roman times
I can hear
The bubbling of the baths
The people rhyme as they want their attention
The horses hooves as they run past

I am travelling back in Roman times
I can smell
The blood of the dead men
The rotten smell of the baths
The horses' poo

I am travelling back in Roman times
I can touch
The swords as they get into battle
The Roman armour as they put it on
The mosaics as we gently put them up.

Emma Johnston (7)
St Philomena's Primary School, Orpington

Tudor Times

The rich people playing skittles with a ball,
Sometimes playing in the great hall.
In the church the bells rings,
And the choir can loudly sing.
The old man is ringing a bell
And the street has a disgusting smell.
Henry VIII receiving his coronation hat,
By his sixth wife, he's a little fat!
Rich Tudors hunting fish or meat,
Poor begging in the street

Simon Lesniakowski (9)
St Philomena's Primary School, Orpington

On The Train To Safety

As I help my brother with his heavy case
To the seat we race
The one nearest my mum
She calls, 'Have fun,
Eat your greens and say your prayers,
Look after your brother and his teddy bears.'
The whistle, I wave goodbye.
I promised myself I wouldn't cry.
My teacher begins to nag,
She gives us all a name tag.
London is gone,
Cries are replaced by birdsong.
You must think I'm barking mad,
But in a way I'm glad.
We drive past crystal green grass,
Woolly, white monsters cross our path.
I take a deep breath as the train pulls in,
It is easy to squeeze out, rations make us thin.
Now in the country, on a farm,
No more air raid alarm.

Charlotte Raven-Shorey (10)
St Philomena's Primary School, Orpington

Roman Rhyme

As I travel back in time,
Back to Roman rhyme.
Chariots racing around
People fighting
People playing music
Food cooking
Wine being served
Romans suffering
Cheers of people
As I travel back in time, back to Roman rhyme
The cold armour
The soft feel of a horse.

Jasmine Booker (7)
St Philomena's Primary School, Orpington

My Life In WWII

I was sleeping calmly, dreaming away,
I was woken by an annoying siren,
The noise was so strong that I felt it.
Bombs pouring down like rain,
I went to the air raid shelter,
Scalding water burning me,
I felt my blood turn cold.
The fire was crackling with sadness.
Mum was carrying me to the countryside,
I saw my dad soaring across the moonlit sky.
All I saw was dust and soot,
My feet were cold,
I was living in horror,
I despair.
My death was waiting for me,
Crashing noises,
I heard nothing but silence.
I went out,
Standing in a wasteland country,
Death was calling, death was calling . . .

Emily Nguyen (10)
St Philomena's Primary School, Orpington

Angry Romans

If I was a Roman
I'd see a bubbling bath
Romans saying 'Rah!'
People dead on the floor.

If I was a Roman
I'd hear screams of people falling off horses
Soldiers munching on hard food
People crying in the amphitheatre

If I was a Roman
I'd feel the armour, I'd touch the shiny swords
Water coming out of the fountain.

Emily McMahon (7)
St Philomena's Primary School, Orpington

When I Fought A Roman

When I fought a Roman
I could see
Big, tough armour
Tall amphitheatre
Patterned buildings

When I fought a Roman
I could hear
Bubbles popping
Brave gladiators fighting
The crowd cheering

When I fought a Roman
I could smell
Smelly, rotten eggs
A huge fire
Salty sea

When I fought a Roman
I could touch
Big, shiny swords.

Gregory Stevens (8)
St Philomena's Primary School, Orpington

A Man In The Blitz

The ground is shaking beneath my body,
I cannot feel my feet.
People screaming like never before,
But I am shaking.
All I can think of is my son and my wife,
All I can see is the bright blue sky, full of planes
And my house shattering to pieces.
The sound of soldiers and fire,
Men screaming,
The fire sizzling.
Sirens and bombs,
I'm turning paler by the minute,
My heart stopped beating, I'm not in it.

Kenneth Renaldo Alexander Jonson (10)
St Philomena's Primary School, Orpington

Through The Roman Past

Through the Roman past
I can see the splish splash of the naked Romans
Chatting and swimming underwater,
Torch flames swaying,
Fountains spitting out tiny drops of water.

Through the Roman past
I can hear the munch, crunch of people
Chewing grapes in their palace,
People jeering in the stadium,
People riding carts on the bumpy street.

Through the Roman past
I can smell the fruit in the crowded market place,
The steaming water where the naked Romans have their baths,
People selling food in the Roman stadium.

Through the Roman past
I can touch the fruit in a huge Roman palace,
The rosemary on its long stem.

Nnenna Okoro (8)
St Philomena's Primary School, Orpington

A Soldier in WWII

I can feel the fear in the soldiers.
Louder than I can hear,
Buildings on fire,
Jets even higher,
Vibrations of guns,
Heavy breathing from lungs,
Dripping sweat,
Grenades you always get,
Dust and dirt in your hair,
Guns louder than the roar of a bear,
Speeding hearts beating,
Strict generals leading,
Screaming orders
And people bleeding.

Nathan Rowan Thomas (10)
St Philomena's Primary School, Orpington

The Romans

I can see,
A spouting fountain,
Naked Romans bathing,
People talking,
The bubbling water,
The colourful tiles.

I can hear,
People shouting,
People sighing,
People cheering.

I can smell,
The fire's flames burning,
The stinky bathers.

I can touch,
The statues,
The metal armour.

Nicole Jimoh (7)
St Philomena's Primary School, Orpington

1939 - The Day It All Began

1939, the day it all started.
Soldiers risking their lives,
Dads and daughters parted.
Death awaits many people,
Hearts begin to pound,
Children running into air raid shelters,
Bombs falling to the ground.
Many people crying,
The flames bursting out with anger,
Lots of people dying,
The hearts of soldiers gone!
Hundreds of Spitfires zooming through the sky,
Wild monsters dropping from the air.
But wait!
I wave my mum goodbye.

Ekiyor Emukpoeruo (11)
St Philomena's Primary School, Orpington

A Child In WWII

I can see broken homes,
Bombs on the floor ready to explode!
Black smoke from fires,
Misty smoke everywhere in the sky.
People running for their lives,
People being evacuated to the country.
I can hear loud sirens,
Planes in the sky,
Bombs dropping,
Soldiers shooting,
People shouting.
Terrified children crying, screaming,
I feel scared.
I can feel my heart pounding with fear.
The vibrations of bombs
Dropping hard on the ground,
Ready to explode!

Kali Louise Aungier (11)
St Philomena's Primary School, Orpington

Back To The Romans

Back in the Roman times
I can see people splashing each other in a hot bath
And some people relaxing.

Back in the Roman times
I can hear cheering and shouting in the battle arena
While bashing swords.

Back in the Roman times
I can smell fresh bread being made
And other sorts of food.

Back in the Roman times
I can touch the rope of a carriage
And if you fall off maybe you can hold onto
The wood at the back.

Samuel Jacobs (7)
St Philomena's Primary School, Orpington

Tudor Times

What can I see?
I can see the queen being crowned
And see her lovely gown.

What can I smell?
I can smell a bonfire
And herbs.

What can I taste?
I can taste the feast
And market food.

What can I hear?
I can hear talking
And music.

What can I feel?
I feel happy and excited
Because the Queen is being crowned.

Ellie Copeland Evans (8)
St Philomena's Primary School, Orpington

Romans' Lives

In through the field of dead Romans I go
Naked Romans washing their bodies
The beautiful Roman statues in the temple
Water fountain splashing on me

Through the field of horses I go along
The screaming of gladiators fighting
With serious Romans trying to kill him

Through the old Roman path I go
Rotten eggs flowing everywhere
Salty sea going through my nose

Along the old Roman path
Hard rock
The metal armour.

Selma Frimpong (7)
St Philomena's Primary School, Orpington

A Woman In Need

Death is waiting,
Cold-hearted murder,
Is this the Britain I know?
Sorrow drumming beside me,
I must leave.

Bombing above me,
Sickness is coming,
Hearts of evil,
Crying of babies,
Crying of mothers,
I must go.

Rough dirt,
Icy smoke brushes my hair,
Death is crawling,
My heart skips a beat.

Semedyong Afangide (11)
St Philomena's Primary School, Orpington

Roman Life

I can see -
Naked Romans in the baths,
Red flames wiggling and dancing,
Fire in the red light,
A green bath with bubbles,
A water fountain with spitting water,
The steam of the pool.

I can hear -
Fighting in the amphitheatre and cheering
The talking of the Romans
My Roman I cheered for has won!

I can smell -
The horse poo in the field
The blood of someone,
Roman breath.

Mia Cutts (7)
St Philomena's Primary School, Orpington

Tudor Times

Tudors everywhere . . .
Queens getting married
Queens getting divorced
Queens getting beheaded
Queens die

Tudors everywhere . . .
Tudors are dirty and smelly
Tudors eating soup and stew

Tudors everywhere . . .
Tudor servants cooking
Tudor Henry eating
Tudor lords and ladies dancing
Tudor palace posh/

Jessica Austin (8)
St Philomena's Primary School, Orpington

Tudor Kitchen

What I can see -
I can see rats everywhere,
I can see the butcher sharpening his axe.

What I can hear -
I can hear the butcher sharpening his axe.

What I can smell -
I can smell the roasting pork for King Henry.

What I can taste -
I can taste the cold air and herbs and spices.

What I can feel -
I can feel the jet-black smoke hitting against me.

Daisy Ashley-Barrett (8)
St Philomena's Primary School, Orpington

Tudor Times

What can I hear?
I hear people talking and feet passing by.

What do I smell?
I smell the bread in the bakery.

What can I feel?
I can feel the wind on my face.

What do I see?
I see people busy at work and ladies in fancy clothes.

What do I taste?
I taste the bitter air.

Olivia Sparkes (8)
St Philomena's Primary School, Orpington

I Would Rather Be At School

My name is Charlie and I am six years old,
I am always hungry and cold.

My master is nasty and so mean,
He makes me sweep the chimneys clean.

I climb up in the dark and soot,
I am dirty from head to foot.

I am so scared that I will fall
And wish that I could go to school.

Robyn Codali (9)
St Philomena's Primary School, Orpington

Tudor Times

T aken to the Tudor time, it could be very tense
U nderground sewage holes? Obviously none of them!
D eath, divorce, beheadings, would Henry ever stop?
O wners of this palace must have been very posh
R ight back to the Tudors reign, it'll never be seen again.

Zack Teale (9)
St Philomena's Primary School, Orpington

Life In Victorian Times

V ery hard working coal miners
I cy cold from no heating
C heerful, even though life was hard
T errified of dangerous explosions
O ld, worn out clothes tattered, in rags
R ail tracks just been laid
I nventors created the motor car and telephone
A ge of steam and steel
N ow life is beginning to look good.

Thomas Sealey (9)
St Philomena's Primary School, Orpington

Flying In Fear

We take off the runway,
I'm trembling in fear as we know we might die today.
We take a gulp, off we go.
Four minutes into the flight
We get into a live firefight with the Germans.
We shot some down.
There were too many,
In fear of dying we turned back,
Knowing we will live another day.

Dominic Johnson (10)
St Philomena's Primary School, Orpington

Victorians

They were really sobby because they had no hobbies.
They had no fun because there were things to be done.
They could not climb because they did not have the time.
They could be very ill but they hated a chill.
When they're very ill and they say 'Hi.'
A few minutes later they could die.

Liam Boyd (9)
St Philomena's Primary School, Orpington

Henry And Wives!

Henry sent out explorers,
Then he became an adorer,
Horrid Henry and agile Anne wedded,
Then agile Anne got beheaded,
Soon he had a new wife,
But she didn't like her new life,
His new wife Anne of Cleves,
Looked like a horse,
So he got a divorce,
Catherine Howard was next,
She was quite a test,
Only a two year reign,
Then her neck got the pain,
Catherine Parr was last,
Now the others are past,
And Henry is dead,
But he didn't lose his head.
Now my story is done - hooray!

Lily Velecky (8)
South Malling CE Primary School, Lewes

The Wife Who Died

Watch beefy Henry stride
It's almost as if he was hiding a knife
Horror Henry had six wives
Sadly one of them died
But the last one survived!
Henry really loved the wife who died
So when his second wife's head landed on the ground with a plop
Henry galloped off feeling like he could pop
To find the wife who died
In the distance is The Tower of London,
Which has a damp dark dungeon
The wife who died was not mean
But she was very clean
Even though she wasn't really seen.

Hannah Poulter (8)
South Malling CE Primary School, Lewes

Message From The Heart To The Heart Scarab

Don't tell I stole my mum's sticky, gooey and oozing fudge brownies!
Don't tell I knocked over Big Ben, it made a loud noise!
Don't tell I smashed the massive, lion-headed golden sphinx!
Don't tell I stole Prince Arthur's dazzling, shimmering, shining, silver and golden sword.
Don't tell I stole the ruby-red diamond from the Queen's royal room!
Don't tell I became the king today!
Don't tell I tripped over the Queen!
Don't tell I rode a new golden motorbike to school.
Don't tell I rode on my mum's roof of her car!
Don't tell I rode a T-rex to school!
Don't tell I ran down the corridor I got told off by the head teacher!
Don't tell I stole Mrs Geering's coffee cup!
Don't tell I stole my dad's car!
Don't tell I smashed my mum's most lovely cup!

Alex Brydon (8)
South Malling CE Primary School, Lewes

The Chop

Anne Boleyn is getting the chop
come and see her get the chop
see her head drop
on the muddy ground
come and see the gory blood
the blood is like a small flood
you hear a deafening sound
that will make a tiger pound
and make a human drop its pound
so roll up, roll up, roll up
Anne Boleyn is getting the chop.

Liam Brown (8)
South Malling CE Primary School, Lewes

Message From The Heart To The Heart Scarab

Don't tell I had three oozing, creamy fudge brownies instead of two.
Don't tell I let a silver baby shark into a swimming pool.
Don't tell I stole a lightsaber from Luke Skywalker.
Don't tell that I put fake black spiders on my mum's computer!
Don't tell I brought Big Ben into school.
Don't tell I swapped Brazil for Madagascar!
Don't tell when I went in a submarine I saw Predator X (a sea dinosaur).
Don't tell I stole Cleopatra's viper.
Don't tell I ripped Egypt off the map.
Don't tell I jumped into the little green helicopter on my watch and flew away.

Alex Massie (7)
South Malling CE Primary School, Lewes

Message From The Heart To The Heart Scarab

Don't tell I pulled clouds from the pyramids in Egypt.
Don't tell I drank too much fizzy pop and it made
my tummy queasy.
Don't tell I hid my teacher's pink sparkly coffee cup.
Don't tell I swung through the hot sticky jungle with Mowgli.
Don't tell I threw a shiny orange ball through my mum's
kitchen window.
Don't tell I played catch with Baloo the bear.
Don't tell I jumped so high on my trampoline that I flew through the air
And landed on my parent's favourite prickly bush.

Callum Baker (7)
South Malling CE Primary School, Lewes

Message From The Heart To The Heart Scarab

Don't tell . . . I put cream on my dad's nose.
Don't tell . . . I soaked my dad's T-shirt in honey.
Don't tell . . . I stole Sleeping Beauty's enchanted ruby-red rose.
Don't tell . . . I ate all the chocolates on my Christmas tree!
Don't tell . . . I drank too much fizzy pop and it made my tummy queasy!
Don't tell . . . I slid off a T-rex's tail!

Ellie Norledge (8)
South Malling CE Primary School, Lewes

My Friend Had A Dream

My friend had a dream
her dream was about a Queen
the Queen was always her of course
but she did not know that she looked like a horse
then a parcel
came to her castle
the parcel was from Henry
and when she read the letter she thought he was very friendly
he wrote on the letter that he wanted to marry her
so she sent a letter back saying, yes Sir, yes Sir.

Mia Fullerton McIntyre (9)
South Malling CE Primary School, Lewes

Message From The Heart To The Heart Scarab

Don't tell I slid down tangled long silky hair.
Don't tell I jumped on my homework.
Don't tell I knocked down the school building.
Don't tell I danced on a car roof.
Don't tell I stole every single biscuit from the school cupboard.
Don't tell I rode a fierce dragon to school.
Don't tell I kidnapped the soft star from the
'Twinkle Twinkle Little Star' song.
Don't tell I took Tutankhamun's death mask.

Tara Allen (7)
South Malling CE Primary School, Lewes

Anne Boleyn Is Ready For The Show

Do you want to see Anne's head chopped off?
Roll up, roll up for the show take your places for the show
To go and play the game.
Ready, steady, go, chop, chop goes the axe and
Anne's head fell down.
The blood dribbled down next to a pile of mud
The crowd goes crazy.

Amy Light-Johnson (8)
South Malling CE Primary School, Lewes

Message From The Heart To The Heart Scarab

Don't tell I was the one who crashed a speeding Red Arrow.
Don't tell I took all the crunchy, tasty Bourbon biscuits from Waitrose.
Don't tell I ordered a humungous passenger hovercraft from B&Q.
Don't tell I sneaked out of my cosy bed and watched TV!
Don't tell it was me who knocked down the school building!
Don't tell I hacked and axed the Big Bad Wolf at Grandma's cottage.
Don't tell it was me who blew Hurricane Katrina across the deep and sparkling blue sea.

Charlie Allen (7)
South Malling CE Primary School, Lewes

Message From The Heart To The Scarab

Don't tell I stole Mum's expensive lipstick.
Don't tell I kissed my black and white two-year-old puppy.
Don't tell I squirted tomato ketchup all over my mum.
Don't tell I turned into beautiful Cleopatra.
Don't tell I've seen Father Christmas.
Don't tell I'm Garfield's owner.
Don't tell I jumped off a ten metre high diving board
Into freezing Enigma ice cream.

Niah Salmon (7)
South Malling CE Primary School, Lewes

King Henry

King Henry not so friendly
Trudged down the street with his legs so bendy.
He had six wives
Three of which lost their lives.
Two lost their lives on the chopping block.
I don't think they needed a doc.
Three got divorced and moved away.
One lived till she was old and died a natural way.

Phoebie Jupp (8)
South Malling CE Primary School, Lewes

Message From The Heart To The Heart Scarab

Don't tell I slid off a T-rex tail.
Don't tell I played chess with a T-rex.
Don't tell I cuddled the pyramid at Giza.
Don't tell I stole Tutankhamun's tomb.
Don't tell I knocked down the huge pyramid at Giza.
Don't tell I burst a hot air balloon with a pin.
Don't tell I put death mask on my brother!
Don't tell I ate the last chocolate cake.

Holly Taylor (7)
South Malling CE Primary School, Lewes

Message From The Heart To The Heart Scarab

Don't tell I built a house out of tasty, red lollies.
Don't tell I put jam in my mum's shoes.
Don't tell I jumped into a LEGO red racer's book.
Don't tell I hugged the world.
Don't tell I was the one who stole Van Gogh's paintings.
Don't tell I bought a whole box of ice lollies.
Don't tell I counted to a trillion!

Lewis McIver (7)
South Malling CE Primary School, Lewes

Message From The Heart To The Heart Scarab

Don't tell I turned into Tutankhamun's wrapped mummy at night.
Don't tell I turned into glorious Cleopatra.
Don't tell I stole Mrs O'Donoghue's golden jewels and put them under her pillow.
Don't tell I rode a huge dinosaur to school!
Don't tell I jumped off the manky grey London Bridge with only a swimming costume!
Don't tell I rode a silver shiny motorbike in Mrs O'Donoghue's office!

Arwyn-Rose James (8)
South Malling CE Primary School, Lewes

Message From The Heart To The Heart Scarab

Don't tell I put make-up on my dad when he was sleeping.
Don't tell I jumped out of an aeroplane and landed in a pool.
Don't tell I broke the rickety-rackety thin bridge.
Don't tell I ate all the chocolates on the bright green bushy Christmas tree.
Don't tell I played tennis with a scaly angry T-rex.
Don't tell that I stole Little Red Riding Hood's cloak.
Don't tell I threw the moon away.

Polly Cowper (8)
South Malling CE Primary School, Lewes

Message From The Heart To The Heart Scarab

Don't tell that I got a load of sugar and ate it.
Don't tell that I stole a fiver.
Don't tell that I stole a red Ferrari.
Don't tell that I robbed Tutankhamun's tomb.
Don't tell I stole the number one.
Don't tell that I stole Hitler's tiny black moustache.
Don't tell that I grabbed a gold shiny star.

Louis Harris (7)
South Malling CE Primary School, Lewes

The Death Of Anne Boleyn

Roll up, roll up, roll up
Anne Boleyn is getting the chop.
Blood goes everywhere,
There's only one hour to go so get your tickets for the show.
Roll up, roll up, roll up, roll up
To see Anne's head come off.
See Anne finished with a chop.

Abigail Coley (8)
South Malling CE Primary School, Lewes

Message From The Heart To The Heart Scarab

Don't tell I stole my mum's red expensive lipstick.
Don't tell I ate a really big, hot, delicious chocolate cake.
Don't tell I hid my lovely, strong big dog.
Don't tell I've got 100 Labrador puppies.
Don't tell I covered my big house in sticky gooey honey.
Don't tell I brought big, strong Baby Bear into school.
Don't tell I took one of the stars from Hollywood.

Keira McTernan (7)
South Malling CE Primary School, Lewes

The Terrible Things About Henry

Horrid Henry wasn't very friendly
from the dead of Anne Boleyn's head
blood flew everywhere up, down through the air.
Henry did not care the crowd was cheering,
'We don't care, we don't care.'
'Anne Boleyn is dead,'
'Yay the world is free.'

Megan Bliss (8)
South Malling CE Primary School, Lewes

Message From The Heart To The Heart Scarab

Don't tell I stole every biscuit at school.
Don't tell I saw Father Christmas.
Don't tell I took all the chocolate ice cream from my freezer.
Don't tell I put on my mum's make-up and I looked really funny.
Don't tell I knocked my dad's chocolates off the cupboard onto the floor.
Don't tell I danced over the sparkling rainbow.

Maisie Notley (7)
South Malling CE Primary School, Lewes

Message From The Heart To The Heart Scarab

Don't tell I spent my dinner money on melted dark chocolate.
Don't tell I turned off all the street lights.
Don't tell I glued my teacher's bottom to her red chair.
Don't tell I painted my mum's pillow pink.
Don't tell I stole the wolf's black fierce big tooth.
Don't tell I stole the Christmas carol and threw it in the bin.

Macey Read-Johnson (8)
South Malling CE Primary School, Lewes

Message From The Heart To The Heart Scarab

Don't tell I threw strawberry yoghurt at my brother.
Don't tell I saw Father Christmas!
Don't tell I spent my dinner money on sweets.
Don't tell I wore my red school uniform in the Bonfire Parade.
Don't tell I stole the bride's dress.

Myles Govus (7)
South Malling CE Primary School, Lewes

River Nile

The River Nile is a gentle, calm and flowing river.

As the wind gradually got wild like a storm; but it settled down
and just started to blow like a glorious breeze making me cooler.

It flows like the crystal, blue ocean shining in the glistening sun
glowing like a diamond in the sky.

You can swim or take your boat out on the humongous river
like you are all alone and just seeing the pyramids and the slaves sweating.

Also you could just fall asleep as the waves make a magnificent
and beautiful noise.

As well as the pharaoh's horse's shoes as they trot into the orange sunset.

It is as important as a pharaoh's jewels underneath the pyramid shining
as well as blinding you.

Katie Bennison (8)
Westcourt Primary School, Gravesend

My Roman Poem

(Based on 'The Sound Collector' by Roger McGough)

A stranger called this morning
Dressed all in black and grey
Put every sound in a bag
And carried them away.

The rattling of the silver coins
The chipping of the special mosaics being made
The weeping of the poor people
As they search for food.

The screaming of the gladiator getting killed
The splashing of the drop from the baths
The chatting of the gladiators
As they plan.

The cheering of the happy crowd
The splashing of the drop from the baths
The chatting of the gladiators
As they plan.

The cheering of the happy crowds
The stomping of the army going to war
The crunching of the Romans as they eat and
As they drink.

A stranger called this morning
He didn't leave his name
Left us only silence
Life will never be the same.

Makayla Samuel (7)
Westcourt Primary School, Gravesend

Egyptian Senses

I see a hard pyramid catch the light in the sun.
I see poor slaves carrying dusty, scorching rocks.
I feel hot sand zooming around.
I feel bursting soil, rusty from pulling.
I hear a cat growling and scratching.

Lacey Rainford (8)
Westcourt Primary School, Gravesend

The Sound Collector

(Based on 'The Sound Collector' by Roger McGough)

A stranger called this morning
Dressed all in black and grey
Put every sound into a bag
And carried them away

The crashing of the gladiators' red, yellow, brown shields
The squeaking of the chariots' wooden, black wheels
The rattling of the slinky, silver coins
As they bounce in the soldiers' pockets

The arguing of the rich men in the tepidarium
The shouting of the dirty, sweaty gladiators
The grumbling of the angry, poor slaves
The cheering of the excited crowd
As they watch people do chariot racing.

The chipping of the hard mosaics being made
The weeping of the poor, poor people
As they search for delicious food

A stranger called this morning
He didn't leave his name
Left us only silence
Life will never be the same.

Elizabeth Olowoyeye (7)
Westcourt Primary School, Gravesend

Egyptian Senses

I see gigantic, looming pyramids with gods to protect him,
his name is Tutankhamun.

I also see pyramids almost touching the daylight and I see hot scorching sand rustling up against the pyramids.

I hear slaves' feet dragging in the hot, scorching sand by the
River Nile that is the hottest place ever.

I feel the slimy, gooey brain wiggling on my hand like a pile of worms from the dry mud, also it feels like I am going to eat it, yuck!

Elizabeth Parker (8)
Westcourt Primary School, Gravesend

The Roman Poem

(Based on 'The Sound Collector' by Roger McGough)

A stranger called this morning
Dressed all in black and grey
Put every sound into a bag
And carried them away.

The clashing of the gladiators' gold swords
The chipping of the huge special mosaics being made
The cheering of the excited crowd
As they watch the chariots zoom by.

The screaming of the young pretty ladies being chased
The squeaking of the old rusty chariot's wheels
The rattling of the gold, silver and bronze coins
As they bounce in the emperor's brown pockets.

The shouting of the excited people watching the dirty gladiators fight
The grumbling of the angry dirty slaves
The weeping of the poor hungry humans
As they search for food.

A stranger called this morning
He didn't leave his name
Left only silence
Life will never be the same.

Brooklyn Flello (7)
Westcourt Primary School, Gravesend

Zeus

As powerful as the ocean's current Zeus the mighty god of all gods!

Controls the heavens like lots of surveillance cameras surveying the area.

He carries his lightning bolt ever so proud.

Ruled the gods like a lion ruling his territory.

Two brothers one as evil as ten devils put together
And the other as intelligent as a teacher.

Powerful towards the weather and it changes very often.

Jordan Niblett (10)
Westcourt Primary School, Gravesend

The Roman Poem

(Based on 'The Sound Collector' by Roger McGough)

A stranger called this morning
Dressed all in black and grey
Put every sound into a bag
And carried them away

The banging of the silver shield
The chirping of the Romans making a brick house
The crackling of the Romans making a bridge
As they chat

The tearing of the toddlers breaking some laurel wreath
The moaning of the slaves
The cheering of the crowd
As they fight

The rattling of the money in the soft pockets
The squeaking of the chariot wheels
The clicking of the horse
As they travel to Rome

A stranger called this morning
He didn't leave his name
Left us only silence
Life will never be the same.

Irie Ives (7)
Westcourt Primary School, Gravesend

The Nile

I am swimming along the River Nile; I can see the fish swimming under me.
I can see the waves ahead coming to me.
I see a boat with slaves in coming to me.
I can hear the whistling wind blowing across the River Nile.
I can hear the water smashing against the rocks.
I can hear other people swimming past me
Also I can hear fish zooming past other people.
I feel very worried because a boat with slaves in might hit me.
Despite the fact I am worried I feel happy because the fish are under me.

William Bayliss (8)
Westcourt Primary School, Gravesend

The Roman Poem

(Based on 'The Sound Collector' by Roger McGough)

A stranger called this morning
Dressed all in black and grey
Put every sound into a bag
And carried them away

The chipping of the special mosaic being made
The banging of the metal tools
The crashing of the gladiators' silver shields
As they hit together.

The splashing of the children in the baths
The grumbling of the dirty soldiers
The weeping of the poor people
As they search for food.

The cheering of the noisy crowd
The squeaking of the brown wooden wheels
The rustling of the laurel wreath
As the wind blows it.

A stranger called this morning
He didn't leave his name
Left us only silence
Life will never be the same.

Madison Flello (7)
Westcourt Primary School, Gravesend

Poseidon

Poseidon, god of earthquakes and sea, causing whirlpools when he is angry.
Protector of sailors and ships, guiding them through waves back to shore.
Proud Poseidon lives in an underwater palace.
He holds a glowing, gleaming, golden trident.
Brother of honour and evil.
Sailors have to worship him.
He sends shipwrecks when he is really cross!
Diving dolphins dazzling through the water waiting to be stroked by Poseidon.
His underwater palace holds lots of gold like a colossal treasure chest.

Karandeep Singh Saluja (11)
Westcourt Primary School, Gravesend

A Stranger Called This Morning

(Based on 'The Sound Collector' by Roger McGough)

A stranger called this morning
Dressed all in black and grey
Put every sound into a bag
And carried them away

The screaming of the dirty Roman people getting killed
The shouting of the rusty gladiators fighting
The crashing of the gladiators' golden shields
As they bash into each other

The rustling of the huge standards swaying side to side
The chipping of the amazing mosaics being made
The cheering of the excited crowd
As they watch the speeding chariots

The banging of the wooden hammer banging
The rumbling of the mad slaves
The weeping of the poor people
As they find some food

A stranger called this morning
He didn't leave his name
Left us only silence
Life will never be the same.

Lauren Stammers (8)
Westcourt Primary School, Gravesend

Zeus

Zeus was the powerful king of the god.
Zeus is in charge of Olympus.
Zeus has a power of thunder also controls the weather.
Zeus as dangerous as a thunderbolt
Zeus' symbols are eagle, oak tree, thunderbolt and lightning bolt.
Playfully like a fighter with brother.
The good fighter like a champion wrestler.
Zeus rules all gods like Pluto, Hera, Trades, Demeter, Ares, Poseidon, Hermes,
Artemis, Dionysus, Apollo, Athena, Aphrodite, Hesston.

Pardeep Sharrma (10)
Westcourt Primary School, Gravesend

The Romans Sound Poem

(Based on 'The Sound Collector' by Roger McGough)

A stranger called this morning
Dressed all in black and grey
Put every sound into a bag
And carried them away

The squeaking of the chariot's wooden wheels
The banging of the Romans building roads and bridges
The crashing of the strong men
As they were being pushed together.

The chipping of the people making a pretty mosaic
The shouting of the angry, dirty gladiators fighting
The cheering of the people cheering
As they went to the finish line.

The rattling of the gold coins
The weeping of the people looking for food

A stranger called this morning
He didn't leave his name
Left us only silence
Life will never be the same.

Sileena Ann Farrell (7)
Westcourt Primary School, Gravesend

A Stranger Called This Morning

(Based on 'The Sound Collector' by Roger McGough)

A stranger called this morning
Dressed all in black and grey put
The grumbling of the slaves walking
The rattling of the money
The clinching of the Romans' swords
The splashing of the man as
He stepped in the bath
The stomping of the Romans
The banging of the shields
The grumbling of the slaves.

Alisha Eastwood (7)
Westcourt Primary School, Gravesend

The Victorian Classroom

Damp desk
Lays anxiously
Dusty blackboard
Rotten benches
Sit happily
Glistening bells
Rings loudly
Lonely basket
Waiting sadly
Filthy oil lamps
Burn crossly
Dirty pictures
Stand quietly
Huge timetable
Hang safely
Smelly bin
Cries sadly
Wooden abacus
Stares lazily.

Saffron Fothergill (9)
Westcourt Primary School, Gravesend

A Stranger Called This Morning

(Based on 'The Sound Collector' by Roger McGough)

A stranger called this morning
Dressed all in black and grey
Put every sound into a bag and carried them away
The rustling of the laurel wreaths
As they are being made
The gladiators' silver and yellow swords
As they are carried into battle
The gladiators as they go chariot racing
The clashing of the gladiators' golden shields
The splashing of the brave Romans
The shouting of the arrows fight
The squeaking of the wooden silver wheels.

Alicia Stickells (7)
Westcourt Primary School, Gravesend

My Egyptian Senses

I see the giant, looming, gold pyramids which almost touch the deep blue sky.

Also, slaves dragging their sandy, smelly feet to carry the huge, disgusting stones.

Next, I see the famous pharaoh Tutankhamun who was buried
in the sand.
I find out that two men found some buried treasure under a tomb.

I hear the River Nile floating over the rocks and over the waterfall to the end of the river.
Then I hear the king of Egypt ordering to his slaves to
go fetch more stones!

I feel the slimy heart being disgustingly put into the canopic jar and I feel the silky sand swaying down the pyramids.

I see the cat licking his paws and growling at his shadows.
Then I could see the River Nile floating across the waves and over the silky sand.

I hear the slaves whispering in the wind.
Next I hear the slaves peering in the hot, sunny wind.

Bethany Norman (8)
Westcourt Primary School, Gravesend

I Want To See . . .

I want to see the very famous River Nile, everyone uses the River Nile.
Why can't I?

Also the River Nile floats down by the deep, dark tomb.

I want to see Tutankhamun because he is a very famous king,
everyone loves him!

I want to see Tutankhamun's gold and try it all on but I don't want to raid it,
just try it on.

Would you like to try it on?

I want to see the giant, looming pyramids that nearly touch the sky
and see what is inside of them.

I want to see the pyramids that look like gold!

Lily-Mae Hall (8)
Westcourt Primary School, Gravesend

The Roman Clatter

(Based on 'The Sound Collector' by Roger McGough)

A stranger called this morning
Dressed all in black and grey
Put every sound into a bag
And carried them away.

The screaming of the Roman people
The squeaking of the chariots' round wheels
As they move around
The shouting of the guards
Standing as straight as a stick.

The rattling of the laurel wreath being made
The stomping of the soldiers going to war.

A stranger called this morning
He didn't leave his name
Left us only silence
Life will never be the same.

Polly Howard (8)
Westcourt Primary School, Gravesend

My Queen Victoria Poem

Golden jewels
Shine brightly
Gleaming orb
Reflects intensely
Twinkling crown
Sparkles happily
Stunning sceptre
Carrying gracefully
Shiny robes
Reaching slowly
Sparkly throne
Glimmers magically
Glorious queen
Lives merrily.

Gary Sandhu (9)
Westcourt Primary School, Gravesend

The Victorian Classroom

Dusty blackboard
Standing proudly
Wooden benches
Rotting slowly
Shiny bell
Tingling quickly
Crumbling desk
Squeaking loudly
Grimy lamp
Shining brightly
Lonely basket
Rocking gently
Dirty fireplace
Warming slowly
Dusty pictures
Blowing quickly.

Keaten Peek (9)
Westcourt Primary School, Gravesend

My Victorian Classroom

Oak benches
Settle tensely
Grimy desks
Rest quietly
Lonely portraits
Stare intently
Chalky blackboard
Teaches frantically
Dusty abacus
Stand lazily
Golden bell
Ring piercingly
Vintage oil lamp
Balances steadily
Straw basket
Rock gently.

Lily Thomas (9)
Westcourt Primary School, Gravesend

A Victorian Classroom

Royal portrait
Stares merrily
Bright lamp
Glistens intensely
Spotless desk
Daydreaming happily
Wooden benches
Stand joyously
Golden bell
Rings noisily
Chalky blackboard
Stands weakly
Wooden abacus
Smiles gracefully
Lonely bin
Smells repeatedly.

Shannon Henzley (9)
Westcourt Primary School, Gravesend

A Victorian Classroom

Golden bell
Rang loudly
Bronze bench
Brightens clearly
Filthy oil lamp
Stands alone
Old basket
Sits lonely
Chalky blackboard
Prominent footing
Wooden abacus
Stared merrily
Huge times tables
Hung safely
Aged fireplace
Daydreams quietly.

Destiny Jackson (9)
Westcourt Primary School, Gravesend

A Victorian Classroom

Filthy oil lamp
Broken daily
Drab pictures
Bend weakly
Dusty blackboard
Stood proudly
Wooden benches
Laying gladly
Dull desks
Burns sadly
Shining abacus
Stared merrily
Murky walls
Crack madly.

Chloe Godfrey (9)
Westcourt Primary School, Gravesend

Tutankhamun's Life

Tutankhamun was a famous pharaoh,
but one day his daddy told him he had to study hieroglyphics.

So he snuck on his golden chariot to race but he had an accident
and had a colossal bump on his head.

He lived for ten more years but then he dropped down dead.

So he got mummified but the slaves saw the bump on his head.

Then they wrapped him up from head to his toes
then they threw him in a pitch-black pyramid.

People kept raiding them so they built a tomb.

After that, nobody ever saw him again
until Howard Carter found all his gold and belongings.

Jack Bundock (8)
Westcourt Primary School, Gravesend

A Stranger Called This Morning

(Based on 'The Sound Collector' by Roger McGough)

A stranger called this morning
Dressed in black and grey
Put every sound into a bag
And carried them away

The booming of the dirty chariots
The chatting of the black slaves
The squeaking of the old wheels

The sploshing of the huge baths
The mopping of the rich Romans
The chatting of the Romans
The blowing of the gladiators.

Sam Bayliss (8)
Westcourt Primary School, Gravesend

Egyptian Senses

I can see the pharaohs sticking the hook up the mummy's nose
and getting the brain out.

I can hear the pencil of the pharaoh writing his name in hieroglyphics.

I can see people racing in their chariots and Tutankhamun on his gold chariot;
he beat the others and came first!
He fell off and had a colossal bump on his head.

When he fell off and had a colossal bump on his head he died
and they made him into a mummy and they put his tomb with him.

The River Nile is red and it is deep
They ride their boat across the River Nile to get some rocks.

The great pyramid is really tall and it is near the River Nile, it is big.

Lewis Henzley (8)
Westcourt Primary School, Gravesend

Queen Victoria

Glorious Queen
Rules affectionately
Resplendent throne
Sits lonely
Elegant robes
Walk gracefully
Stunning jewels
Wander safely
Stands joyously
Sparkling crown
Twinkles above
Glamorous cape
Strolls gladly.

Katie Middleton (9)
Westcourt Primary School, Gravesend

A Stranger Called This Morning

(Based on 'The Sound Collector' by Roger McGough)

A stranger called this morning
Dressed all in black and grey
Put every sound into a bag
And carried them away.

The clash of the golden shields
The bang of the gladiators
The bashing of the fighting in the coliseums.

The shouting of the amphitheatre
The people waiting to fight with gladiators
The sound of the swords banging.

Courtney Collings (7)
Westcourt Primary School, Gravesend

Egyptian Slaves

I see a giant yellow pyramid that is nearly touching the sky
it reminds me of a castle touching the sky.

Also, I see slaves pulling and pulling like a hunter pulling a cage
but the slaves were pulling harder and harder.

I feel some ruby-red, glowing rich jewellery with some lovely patterns
going on and on.

Also I feel some snake faces touching my hands it feels really funny.

I hear fish splashing and splashing along the River Nile
like the waves in the sea.

Also I hear boats crashing along the river too.

Georgina Jarvis (9)
Westcourt Primary School, Gravesend

A Victorian School

Burly benches
Stand inaudibly
Glittering bell
Dazzles brightly
Wooden desks
Relaxes happily
Cold fireplace
Shivered violently
Old lamp
Lights weakly
Chalky blackboard
Waiting silently.

Riley Furness (9)
Westcourt Primary School, Gravesend

A Victorian Classroom

Vintage abacus
Slid gently
Crooked desk
Wobbled constantly
Wooden benches
Sat angrily
Old basket
Stood silently
Chalky blackboard
Stands weakly
Golden bell
Rang loudly.

Malum Shah (9)
Westcourt Primary School, Gravesend

Queen Victoria's Coronation

Charming robes
Drape fabulously
Resplendent throne
Sparkles brightly
Jewelled crown
Glistens magically
Enchanting dress
Reaching endlessly
Gleaming sceptre
Glimmers constantly
Determined Queen
Sits magnificently.

Erin Tree (9)
Westcourt Primary School, Gravesend

A Victorian Classroom

Colourless portraits
Hang gently
Gloomy fireplace
Warms softly
Dusty oil lamp
Flickers constantly
Abandoned ink pen
Sits anxiously
Filthy blackboard
Stands frantically
Glistening bell
Rings loudly.

Cheyenne Irwin (10)
Westcourt Primary School, Gravesend

Hades

Hades is the king, ruling the ghostly underworld with
his dangerous powers.
Hades is always moody and greedy with everybody even
his own brothers.
Hades never listens to anybody so people never listen to Hades.
Hades likes to listen to his guards a lot why can't he
listen to everyone else.
Hades always thinks he's the best in the world.
Hades always shouts out welcome to the pitch-black dark side.
Hades is very bossy all the time.
Hades is never good because he gets into a lot of trouble.
Hades causes chaos all the time in his underground.

Marcus McFarlane (10)
Westcourt Primary School, Gravesend

An Old Victorian Classroom

Wooden basket
Sits sadly
Dirty bins
Cry separately
Old paintings
Frown regularly
White chalk
Writes constantly
Lonely ink pens
Sigh anxiously
Colourless portrait
Hangs gently.

Saran Sesay (9)
Westcourt Primary School, Gravesend

The Victorian Schools

Glorious queen
Dazzling brightly
Glimmering crown
Sparkles endlessly
Shimmering sword
Glittering interesting
Golden sceptre
Twinkles gracefully
Glowing throne
Reaching continuously
Wonderful jewels
Sparkling vividly.

Waynus Eastwood (9)
Westcourt Primary School, Gravesend

The Stranger Called This Morning

(Based on 'The Sound Collector' by Roger McGough)

The stranger called this morning
dressed all in black and grey
every sound was put in a bag and carried them away.

The crashing of the gladiators are driving a dirty car
and they are breaking a dirty wall.
The chirping of the excited prince
loving the princess coming along.
The squeaking of the new shoes.
The weeping of the poor people running for food.
The shouting of the angry people.

Louise Chibnall (7)
Westcourt Primary School, Gravesend

The Roman Poem

(Based on 'The Sound Collector' by Roger McGough)

A stranger called this morning
Dressed all in black and grey
Put his hand in his pocket
And carried them away.

The crash of the gladiators' silver shields
The chipping of the special mosaics being made.

The whining of the poor people
Trying to find food
The cheering of the crowd.

Pippa Stickells (7)
Westcourt Primary School, Gravesend

Artemis

Artemis, goddess of hunting,
sneaks around protecting peaceful animals.
Wearing the sign of the deer,
she creeps around watching the quiet animals
as silent as her shadow.
Caring, loving and a warm place,
Mount Olympus is home to millions of god and goddesses.
Artemis is as silent as the air.
Artemis creeps around as silent as a deer.
She moves quietly and carefully,
no one can hear her.

Lily Fothergill (10)
Westcourt Primary School, Gravesend

Pyramids And Mummies

I see people raiding the pyramids so they built them underground.
I see Egyptians pulling the brain with a sharp and pointy hook from the nose.
I see slaves leaving the heart in the body.
Only rich people can afford mummification.
I see pyramids that touch the sun that shine down on the scorching hot sand.
I hear rustling trees swaying in the wild wind and the water rolling quickly down the river.
I hear slaves dragging their feet across the hot scorching sand.
I feel the heart beating on my hand.
I feel the jelly-like brain slipping and sliding across my hands.
I feel the jelly-like brain slipping and sliding across my hands.

Madison Mckenzie-Baldwin (8)
Westcourt Primary School, Gravesend

I Hear . . .

I hear the River Nile splashing and the wind blowing the dry sand.
I hear the rocks down below the river, scratching the boat.
I hear little waves crashing along the River Nile.
I hear the crumbling pyramid whilst slaves are pushing large stones.

Mary Kate O'Brien (8)
Westcourt Primary School, Gravesend

Hera

Hera, goddess of marriage, she brings happiness to the happy couple,
for many years to come.

Queen of all gods, except one, Zeus, king of them all, even Hera.

Hera, who lives in the heavenly clouds, is also the queen of Heaven.

Hera, Zeus' wife, has two sacred animals.

A peacock to symbolise her beauty, and a cow was very important,
because they sacrificed them for gods.

Marriage is a bright bundle of eternal love, happiness, rings, hearts and roses.

Stephanie Walker (10)
Westcourt Primary School, Gravesend

Zeus

Zeus lord of all gods, powerful, strong, mighty
and kind to the weak and punish the wicked.
Zeus is charming and friendly.
Zeus is as charming as a colourful peacock spreading his feathers.
Zeus' symbols are thunderbolts, oak trees also eagles.
Zeus, the mighty god sends out his magical eagles if there is a message
or a warning if something is happening.
The dignity god, Zeus has had many affairs with mortals behind his wife's back.
He rules all gods such as Hera, Hades, Hermes, Hestia, Hephaestus, Ares,
Apollo, Athena, Aphrodite, Artemis, Demeter, Dionysus and Poseidon.

Jake Jarvis (11)
Westcourt Primary School, Gravesend

Egyptian See, Hear And Feel

I can see the pyramids getting built as the point is in the clouds.

I can see the rich men and women wearing their golden jewels
As it goes in a nice and sweet pattern.

I can see the gigantic footsteps in the sand as they get washed away.

I can hear the waves bring in the sand into the River Nile.

Chelsea Coyne (8)
Westcourt Primary School, Gravesend

A Victorian Poem

Golden sword
Sitting peacefully
Old prince
Posing proudly
Rough robes
Hanging smartly
Shining buttons
Buzzing slightly
Proud medal
Sitting smoothly.

Leroy Stammers (9)
Westcourt Primary School, Gravesend

Prince Albert

Handsome prince
Posing sternly
Shiny sword
Standing delightedly
Curly braid
Hanging tightly
Polished buttons
Twinkle brightly
Cheerful medals
Proudly shining.

Hollie Parker (9)
Westcourt Primary School, Gravesend

Hestia

Hestia, young gentle and pure goddess of the home and hearth.
Like a lamb nice and kind inside, she was like this since her birth.
As Zeus' eldest sister she thought that she had power
But she had to come off of Olympus for good.
She has an enemy, Hades is his name, he shouts off with the head!
His personality don't you know is pure evil of the dead.

Callum Partridge (10)
Westcourt Primary School, Gravesend

A Victorian Classroom

Raised table stood still
Dusty bell lying there
Rotting bench sat alone
Old lamp burning dimly
Tiny desk squeaks loudly
Thin cupboard screwed silent
Blackboard sitting quietly
Gleaming candle resting like a statue
Bright wall stands like a tree
Dull chair sits like a person.

George Greenwood (9)
Westcourt Primary School, Gravesend

Athena

Wild war roars loudly.
Wonderful wisdom helps the old,
Able Athena introduces olive oozing oil.
Holding magnificent Medusa's dead head,
Bright as a light.
A deadly defender!
Glistering grey armour,
Shiny silver symbols.
Able Athena protects cautious cities.
Obedient owls overpower the humans.

Abbie Greenwood (11)
Westcourt Primary School, Gravesend

Hephaestus

Lame as a donkey, Hephaestus the god of fire,
Makes swords and shields for Athena.
Hephaestus is married to Aphrodite the goddess of love and beauty.
He is Zeus' son and Hera is his mother.
He cares for Ares and his other brothers.
His wife fell in love with Eros.

Hayden Jones (10)
Westcourt Primary School, Gravesend

Queen Victoria

Golden throne
Sitting gladly
Glamorous queen
Staring elegantly
Loyal Albert
Watching proudly
Beautiful crown
Sparkling brightly
Long sceptre
Leaning lazily.

Charlie Collings (9)
Westcourt Primary School, Gravesend

A Stranger Called This Morning

(Based on 'The Sound Collector' by Roger McGough)

A stranger called this morning
Dressed all in black and grey
And carried them away

The crashing of the shields
The stomping of the angry soldiers
The splashing of the muddy puddles
As the strong soldiers march
The weeping of the tired slaves.

Lewis Bollen (7)
Westcourt Primary School, Gravesend

Egyptian Senses

I see pyramids that almost touch the sky.
Also sand blowing into the River Nile.
Also I see slaves dragging their feet on the burning hot sand.
I hear people burying the mummies under the pyramids.
I hear pharaohs shouting and giving orders for the slaves.
I feel the pharaoh's brain in my hands like slugs and worms.

Tommy Eden (8)
Westcourt Primary School, Gravesend

A Victorian Queen

Gleaming jewels
Twinkling brightly
Bright gold reflecting
Quickly twinkling crown
Sparkles happily royal
Throne carries gently
Elegant robes hanging
Wildly glorious queen
Live safely.

Jay Hill (9)
Westcourt Primary School, Gravesend

Aphrodite

Aphrodite is the goddess of love and beauty.
Her heart is as warm as the sun in the sky.
She has a shiny gold belt so that you can see people's faces In It.
She was born in the sea and the sea is as blue as the sky.
Doves and sparrows drifted through the wind.
Aphrodite rides upon a scallop.
Dolphins and crabs jump everywhere.
A tree of myrtle growing in an island of shooting sprouts.
Beautiful, dazzling, gorgeous hair waving in the wind.

Grace Toombs (10)
Westcourt Primary School, Gravesend

Dark And Dangerous Classroom

Candles burning
Shining and glittering
Children yawning
In the dark black morning
Children's hats
Like shower caps
Painting pocing
With staring eyes.

Joseph Austen (9)
Westcourt Primary School, Gravesend

Ares

Ares, king of war, bloody, deadly and likes people to die.
Carrying his spear and shield he is bloodthirsty,
Murderous, impulsive and raring for a fight.
Red, death battling fields surround him on Earth.
Dogs and vultures go out to hunt for his enemies to kill!
Ares as vicious as a lion.
Burning torches, dogs and vultures all represent him.

Mason Mckenzie-Baldwin (10)
Westcourt Primary School, Gravesend

The Egyptians

I see a big, enormous pyramid and some more pyramids on the sand.
I see some people and it is hot in Egypt.

Some people live in the pyramid and it is dusty and the people built pyramids a long time ago.

Egyptians put the hooks and get the brain.
The people build pyramids everywhere in Egyptian times.

Dean Watson (8)
Westcourt Primary School, Gravesend

I See, Hear, Feel . . .

I see the River Nile swaying into the bulrushes,
Also slaves building tombs.

I hear the trees swaying also the River Nile splashing
And the wind blowing the burning hot sand.

I feel the Egyptians pulling our brains from the dead kings.

Shane May (8)
Westcourt Primary School, Gravesend

Zeus

A powerful king, Zeus is in charge of Olympus.
Father of the gods he controls the weather.
As strong as a rock throwing at the Minotaur.
Gentle like rubbing a dog.
A good fighter like Medusa.

Charlie Rainford (10)
Westcourt Primary School, Gravesend

Egyptian Senses

I hear the River Nile splashing against the pyramids.
I see the rocks below me waiting to be used in a pyramid.
I feel the sand blowing on me.
I see Tutankhamun's belongings rotting with him as he lays in the tomb.
I smell the cats, they're the Egyptian's favourite animals.

Louis Harvey (8)
Westcourt Primary School, Gravesend

I See . . .

I see giant pyramids.
I see slaves carrying dusty rocks.
I see the scorching sand.
I see damp dusty tombs.
I see Tutankhamun dripping with gold.

Warren Sparks (8)
Westcourt Primary School, Gravesend

I See . . .

I see giant pyramids.
I see slaves carrying dusty rocks.
I see the orange sand.
I see the trees.

Kian Butler (8)
Westcourt Primary School, Gravesend

I See

I see enormous pyramids.
I see slaves carrying dusty rocks.
I see the steaming hot sand.
I see the shiny gold dripping on Tutankhamun.

John Jones (8)
Westcourt Primary School, Gravesend

Egyptian Senses

I see the big tall pyramids in a row and they're almost touching the sky.
Also there are some underground.
I see slaves holding huge rocks.
The pharaoh's tombs are underground so that there is no theft.

Jalal Shah (8)
Westcourt Primary School, Gravesend

Smashing Saxons Travel Back In Rhyme

Saxons' life was really rough,
hanging, stoning and all that stuff,

The Saxons believed in all sorts of things,
like devils and demons,
and all horrible things,

And when there's no food,
they would eat their dead,
and grind their bones,
to make bread.

Ghastly games were always played,
tug of war with
hide of the day.

Saxons caused much bloodshed,
all over the land,
but the Vikings came,
and killed them all to known man.

Bonnie Mai Claxton (10)
Westwood Academy, Hadleigh

One Moment In Time

Travelling through the cyclonic void
like opening a door,
to a time been before.
Time to go to Victorian times,
a place I've only seen in story books and nursery rhymes.
I gaze at the dusty streets
and the chimneys covering the skylight
through the distance the magnificent gleaming
palace stands before me alight.
Where Victoria ruled with a gem-studded crown,
her portrait filled the palace with her infamous frown.
Whilst the hall filled with laughter of the wealthy
with titles and grand names,
this wasn't the case, with the streets filled
with the poor it wasn't same.
The boys climbed the chimneys in houses of the rich,
covered in coal and soot that made them itch,
carts with fruits, for market stalls in the cramped streets
the ladies with weaved baskets full.
The flower stalls brimming with bouquets and stems
the dressmakers, busy sewing skirts, bows and hems.
Kids playing together with shoes, hoops and ropes,
the servants running errands posting small envelopes.
As I leave this fabulous time and place,
let's hurry, come on, no time to waste.
For many historic adventures await us,
the Romans, the Tudors, Georgian times a must.
Take a moment through time and see
with imagination you can go anywhere you want to be.

Rachel Stephens (10)
Westwood Academy, Hadleigh

Henry VIII's Wives

Henry VIII had six wives,
But one gave him a big surprise.

Catherine was number one,
But she failed to give Henry a son,
She divorced and fell to the floor,
She couldn't love Henry anymore.

Next came Anne Boleyn,
They threw her head in a bin,
Anne Boleyn was dreaded,
Before she was beheaded.

Jane Seymour was next at three,
And she was the key,
She gave Henry a son,
It was little Prince Eddie he was the one.

Anne of Cleves was next at four
She had a face like a bore
'No, no, no!' Henry said, 'out of the door.'

Catherine Howard was next at five,
She had a problem to stay alive,
She liked to flirt with other men,
She got her head chopped off again.

Last at six
In 1547 Henry's life came to an end,
That drove Catherine Parr round the bend.

George Barnett & Richard Cook (9)
Westwood Academy, Hadleigh

A Victorian Christmas

Christmas pudding, cards and snow,
Everyone is on the go.
Getting ready for Christmas Day,
Which is only a few days away!

Chestnuts roasting on an open fire,
Turkey hanging on a butcher's wire.
The ghost of Scrooge and Christmas past,
Christmas Day is here at last!

Opening presents is lots of fun,
But if you're poor you don't get one!
All the Christmas bells have rang,
Pulling crackers makes a big bang.

Christmas wreaths on big front doors,
Go to the market to get yours.
Christmas trees tall and green,
Baubles as big as you have ever seen.

A Victorian Christmas is now here,
Everybody wave and cheer.
It's now time to have fun,
'Merry Christmas everyone.'

Rebecca Lacey (8)
Westwood Academy, Hadleigh

The Sounds Of War

Home guard in the city, keeping everyone safe,
Watching, waiting, listening for the air-raid siren song,
'Put that light out,' the warden cries,
'Into the shelter, quick, hurry along.'

Smelling, seeking and finding, whilst playing in the hay,
'Come on kids, it's teatime',
And nearly the end of the day.

The stench in the trench, the mud and the cold,
I have to be brave, I have to be bold.

Finally stepping onto English soil once more,
The sounds of cheers, you just can't ignore.

Flags waving high, like a giant bee,
Seeing all my friends again, it's good to be free!

Michael Dobney (10)
Westwood Academy, Hadleigh

The Tudor King

After his older brother died he was the next in line,
to take the throne and six wives the greedy, greedy man!

Divorced, beheaded and died, divorced, beheaded, survived,
that was the order of all the wives.

Catherine gave him a daughter and the same was given by Anne,
but Jane was the one to give him a son so she was number one.

A short while after his one and only love had gone to Heaven above.

Years went by and at forty-four the king had hurt his leg.
A jousting accident was what it was
and his leg would never mend . . .

Mia Michaela Knight (11)
Westwood Academy, Hadleigh

The Dinosaurs

In the age of the dinosaur,
All you feared was a great big roar!
All the leaves fell off the trees,
Lakes were filled with dino pees!
Tyrannosaurus was the fiercest of all,
Rhamphorhynchus was very small.
Sticks were crunched,
Leaves were munched,
As the dinos ate their lunch.
What a shame they didn't survive,
I wish those dinos were still alive!

Ella Rai Kempton (7)
Westwood Academy, Hadleigh

Horrific Henry The VIII

Henry the VIII how mean,
He was a lean, mean, killing machine,
Well, that sentence was actually true,
Not many people liked him not me nor you,

He had seven wives that's what they say,
Six only had daughters so they had to pay!
Jane Seymour, the only with a son,
She died shortly after which means he only had one.

Catherine of Aragon, Anne Boleyn, Anne of Cleves,
Catherine Howard, Catherine Parr,
There is a rhyme of the order of King Henry the VIII's wives:
Divorced, beheaded, died, divorced, beheaded survived.
Everyone knows that King Henry wasn't very nice,
He was extremely greedy he ate anything including mice!
That's how he died he ate too much food,
No one really cared as to everyone he was crude.

Zoe Pilkington (10)
Woodville Primary School, South Woodham Ferrers

All Hope Is Gone

I have been in the trenches
And sat on the benches

Watched the people being hit
And was beside a man that had nits

My leader carries me until there is a bomb
And I realise all hope is gone.

He dropped me now I see him dead
There's just me now and dead Fred.

A German man is looking at me
Oh no he's taking me.

I'm the gun with no hope . . .

Martin Bowers (10)
Woodville Primary School, South Woodham Ferrers

I Will Be An Astronaut

My name is Neil I am ten.
An astronaut I want to be when,
I am bigger perhaps six feet four.
I will go through that metal door.
I imagine it will shine so bright.
So I will have to keep my eyes shut tight.
There will be celebration all through the night
Just for visiting that little light.

Mitchell Foster (10)
Woodville Primary School, South Woodham Ferrers

Young Writers Information

We hope you have enjoyed reading this book - and that you will continue to enjoy it in the coming years.

If you like reading and writing poetry drop us a line, or give us a call, and we'll send you a free information pack.

Alternatively if you would like to order further copies of this book or any of our other titles, then please give us a call or log onto our website at www.youngwriters.co.uk

Young Writers Information
Remus House
Coltsfoot Drive
Peterborough
PE2 9BF
(01733) 890066